My THOUGHTS *Distilled*

By

Mike Minter

DEDICATION

Dedicated to "Prime Time"
Greatest Sunday school class on planet Earth.

FOREWORD

I first met Mike Minter when I was seventeen years old. We went to the same Bible college, although Mike was a few years my senior. More specifically, we met at a large hotel where we both worked as "runners," parking cars. I knew from the very beginning that Mike had a very special way with people. He was both kind and funny, and even the runners who weren't Christians had a great respect for Mike. He never shied away from sharing his faith, and he was an all-around great example to me!

When Mike left the Bible college to plant a church, I wasn't surprised at all to hear of its progress over the ensuing years. The story of Mike Minter and the church he planted is most interesting, but the fact that Mike pastored the SAME church for over 40 years through every stage of growth, as it grew into a mega-church, is more than interesting. It is mind-boggling! For anyone to stay at the same church for over 40 years is almost unheard of in our day and age. It makes me think of what Charles Spurgeon said when he quipped, "By great perseverance, the snail made it into the ark!"

Perseverance is only one of Mike's many assets! His ability to handle God's Word, added to his ability to captivate an audience, makes for a powerful combination in pastoral ministry. I am thankful that Mike has captured his thoughts in print from his over 50 years of experience. His thoughts cover a wide array of issues, and they will benefit you in a wide array of areas.

Pastoral ministry is not an easy place to live. More and more casualties litter the path a pastor is called to tread. Take encouragement from a pastor who has gone before and come out on the other side, more in love with his Savior than ever before! It can be done! It has been said that every believer needs both a Paul in their lives as well as a Timothy. A mentor as well as a protégé. I offer this book to you as the words of a seasoned pastor to serve as your mentor.

I have known Mike for over 50 years, and I can tell you he is truly a man in whom there is no guile. He is a wealth of wisdom, and any pastor, young or old, will benefit greatly from his years of faithfully mining God's Word for its many treasures. Do yourself a favor, read on, and be blessed!

Joe Allen
Chaplain of Dallas Theological Seminary

PREFACE

The book you are getting ready to engage in is a compilation of many thoughts over many years. There is no theme. There is no narrative leading you to a particular conclusion. There are no thoughts compiled under a particular heading. Perhaps I will do that in volume two. My tendency is that when a new thought enters my very curious mind, I write it down, and then after many months, I compile it into one manuscript, and that is exactly what you will read in *My Thoughts Distilled.* I pray each entry blesses your life as much as I have been blessed in writing it.

Mike

***

Table of Contents

WHY SALVATION MUST BE A GIFT

For God to maintain His integrity, salvation must be offered freely. Let's see why this is the case. If God demands a certain amount of good works to enter heaven, then for Him to be truly honest, He would be required by His own holiness to tell us what those demands are. In other words, He wouldn't just say "be good" without stipulating how good. Otherwise, we would be comparing ourselves to others, trying to figure out on the goodness scale where we fit. That is a frightening thought. This is religion at its best, or should I say at its worst?

Before we get to the good news, we must reckon with God's assessment of human goodness. Paul writes, "There is no one who understands; there is no one who seeks God. All have turned away, they have together become worthless; there is no one who does good, not even one." (Rom 3:11-12).

Years ago, my brother and I were sharing the Gospel with my dad while driving in the car. My dad felt he had lived a good life and would then merit heaven. I posed this question. "From Hitler to Mother Teresa, where on that line do you see yourself?" I think he felt he was 85% good. I then asked him what would happen if he died and found out he needed to be 86% good. He began to panic because he knew no matter what percentage he picked, I would raise the ante. If he picked 90%, I'm going with 95%. Where will this lead? Heaven is perfect, and 99% won't cut it. The 1% of imperfection will pollute God's Kingdom. God never lets good people into heaven; He lets perfect people into heaven.

To leave us stranded by having no idea what He demands in goodness is nothing less than cruel, and God is not cruel. Salvation must be a gift. But we still have not answered the goodness question. Here is the answer: 100% perfection is needed to enter God's perfect Kingdom. What? You read that correctly.

The natural question is, "How do I get that perfection?" As usual, you would expect God to be upfront on how to enter His Kingdom. No guessing, which is frightening, particularly if you guessed wrong. Jesus said, "Unless a man is born again, he cannot enter the Kingdom of God"

(John 3:3). Where do I get the perfection I need to be born again and enter the Kingdom? Here is the clear, unambiguous answer. "God made him who had no sin to be sin in for us so that in him we might become the righteousness of God in Him" (2 Cor. 5:21). Did you catch that? I can be as righteous as God Himself, and that is the perfect righteousness I need to enter His perfect heaven.

This is what is called double imputation. To impute is to put to the account of another. Jesus puts to our account His righteousness, and we put to His account our sin. This is how we gain the perfection to enter heaven. He takes on my sin, and I take on His righteousness. Now that is a good deal. His perfect righteousness is placed to my account as the perfection I need to be born again, leaving the Kingdom of darkness and entering the Kingdom of God's dear Son. But there is a catch. I knew it. There is no free lunch. True, but we are not talking about lunch but eternal life. The Lord beats to death from the Old Testament to the New Testament that man has no inherent righteousness and needs an alien righteousness which is placed to our account when we put our faith in Christ and Christ alone. When this happens, all of Christ's perfection is placed into our account, and we now possess the absolute assurance of where we will spend eternity. That is what the Gospel means. It is not good news to guess if my human goodness will get me into heaven if I have no idea what the standard of goodness is.

So, if salvation is not a gift, then we are in the dark regarding our eternal destiny. This is not the God of the Bible. "For by grace are you saved through faith; and that not of yourselves: it is the gift of God: Not of works, lest any man should boast" (Eph. 2:8-9). How clear can it be?

OBLIGATED VS. ABLE

So often, we believe that if God is able to do something, then He is obligated to do it. We know from experience that this is not true. Consider the people who have not been healed, the jobs that have been lost, and all the prayers that haven't turned out the way those who prayed them had hoped. Failure to understand this leads to great disappointment.

Yes, He is able to heal the marriage. Yes, He is able to bring home the prodigal. But suppose He doesn't? Does this mean that He is not a faithful God? Let's listen in on an Old Testament conversation between Shadrach, Meshach, and Abednego and evil King Nebuchadnezzar as found in the book of Daniel. Three young men were told that if they didn't bow down to the golden image (an idol), they would be thrown into the fiery furnace. Here is their reply to the king: "If we are thrown into the blazing furnace, the God we serve is able to deliver us from it, and he will deliver us from Your Majesty's hand. [18] But even if he does not..." (Dan 3:17-18a).

Note the words "but even if He does not." God's three servants knew He was able, but God had not promised deliverance.

So, herein lies the compelling truth—**God is not obligated to do what He is able to do. He is only obligated to do what He promised to do.** Can He heal you? Most assuredly. Can He restore a marriage? Absolutely. But if not, He is still worthy of our praise. When we confuse what God is able to do with what He has promised to do, we become disillusioned.

So, let's stop telling God what He must do based on His ability and rely only on what He has promised to do. And those promises are found in Scripture. We need to put our hope in Him, not the outcome.

3

TECHNOLOGY AND THE HUMAN HEART

Two hundred years ago, a man went down to catch a stagecoach and just missed it. He asked the ticket agent when the next one would come. The man replied, "Two weeks." Furious at the wait, the traveler headed home. But thank goodness for technological advancement. His son grew up and would never need to ride in a stagecoach. Instead, he went down to the train station but sadly just missed the train. He asked when the next train would arrive. "Two days" was the reply. Frustrated, he headed home. Thank goodness for technological advancement. That man's son wouldn't have to rely on trains but would enjoy the efficiency and swiftness of air travel.

He went down to the airport only to find that he had just missed his flight. He was informed that the next flight was in two hours. "Two hours?!" He stormed off to the airport Starbucks, ordered a latte, and plugged his noise-canceling headphones into his laptop to watch a movie, mitigating the wait. But thank goodness for technology. His son just rolled out of bed and opened his laptop to watch a video that would take two minutes to download. "Two minutes!" Frustrated by the slow connection, he moved on to his phone.

From two weeks to two days to two hours to two minutes—the technology has improved, but the human heart hasn't changed one bit. Technology can't fix the fallen nature of humankind. But we keep trying, don't we? I am not amazed by how much I know about Scripture, but by how much Scripture knows about me. Perhaps this is why the Bible tells us that human eyes are never satisfied (Prov 27:20). Our trust is in the Gospel, which trumps technology.

CRUTCH VS. STRETCHER

How often have you heard a skeptic say that religion is just a crutch? Like it or not, that's a pretty accurate statement. You see, all religions of the world view humanity as having one good leg and one bad leg. Your human ability and goodness are the good leg. The difficulties in your life are the bad leg. Thus, we need outside help from some distant deity. That's what the skeptic calls a crutch. From a skeptical point of view, right on. In addition to personal support, religion often serves as a social structure that offers belonging, community, and identity. For many, being part of a religious group provides a sense of connection and shared purpose. From a skeptic's perspective, this reliance on religion for social support might also be seen as a "crutch," where individuals lean on the comfort of collective beliefs and traditions rather than forging their own independent social identity or philosophy.

However, Scripture never portrays human beings as having one good leg and one bad leg. In John 15:5, Jesus said, "Apart from me, you can do nothing." Somehow, the word "nothing" eliminates the idea of a good leg. He sees us as hopelessly weak. The Apostle Paul reminds us, "There is no one righteous, not even one" (Rom 3:10). There is no crutch because a crutch implies that we have one good leg, which is the mindset of all religious beliefs.

So, we have three views. The view of the skeptic is that I have two good legs and don't need some imaginary god to help me out. The religious view is that I have one good leg and one bad one. Thus, I need a god as my crutch. The biblical view is that I have two bad legs and need new life. In other words, Christianity is not a crutch; it's a stretcher: "For you died, and your life is now hidden with Christ in God" (Col 3:3). So, let's get rid of human reliance and semi-human reliance and climb onto the stretcher. Jesus has two very good legs.

THE ULTIMATE CONTRADICTION

It is my understanding that humankind has about 5,000 years of recorded human history. The combined IQ of the human race is astronomical. We increase in knowledge at an exponential rate. Every couple of years, we double our knowledge in the world of science and technology. Sounds great, but there seems to be a fly in the ointment. It stands to reason that since knowledge is designed to solve problems and knowledge is increasing, then problems should be decreasing at the same rate. But simple observation tells a different story.

In fact, it shows us just the opposite. As knowledge and technology advance, so too does the complexity of the problems we face. While science and technology solve many issues, they often create new, unforeseen challenges. The problems—both locally and internationally—are out of control. We no sooner stamp out one disease than five others take its place. We end one war, and two more ignite. Yet, we are more educated than we have ever been. We know more about dieting than we have ever known, yet that doesn't necessarily translate into health or fitness. We know more about finances than we have ever known, yet debt is commonplace. What's going on here? "For with much wisdom comes much sorrow; the more knowledge, the more grief" (Eccl 1:18).

God is not opposed to knowledge; He is opposed to knowledge replacing God as our Savior. Simple logic tells us that as we increase in knowledge, life should be getting better and better. But God's Word is wiser than human knowledge. He tells us that when our intellectual pride replaces Him as sovereign, then He will turn us over to our own way. "For although they knew God, they neither glorified him as God nor gave thanks to him, but their thinking became futile, and their foolish hearts were darkened. Although they claimed to be wise, they became fools" (Rom 1:21-22).

Between the Word of God and the mind of humanity, daily experience reveals Scripture to be the wiser of the two. Though God loves us, He also knows that we are the source of the problem. Scripture often highlights the limitations of human wisdom compared to divine wisdom. While human knowledge may increase, it cannot fully address deeper moral, spiritual, and existential problems that stem from human nature itself. We are the problem, and when the problem tries to solve the problem, that's a problem.

NO PLACE TO HIDE

Scripture tells us that Jonah fled from the presence of the Lord, yet Psalm 139:7 says we cannot flee from His presence. That Psalm tells us that wherever we go, God is there. So, what's the deal?

Since God is omnipresent (a theological term meaning He is everywhere), then no, we cannot flee from His presence.

However, there is a different type of fleeing. Jonah went as far as he could geographically go to escape the presence of the Lord, but to no avail. God knew all along exactly where he was heading and where he was hiding.

In this instance, when it says that Jonah fled from His presence, it simply means he fled from the moral will of God. He was told to go east, and he headed west. This should both encourage us and warn us at the same time. When we are alone, sin finds its way into our lives more easily than if there are many people watching us. Yet God is always watching, and He is ever-present.

There is a strange twist in our logic when we think we can get away with sin. We think God is too busy keeping the planets in orbit and couldn't possibly see what we are doing. We, like Jonah, flee from His moral will daily. But look where Jonah ended up. Jonah thought that running away from his home meant he could run away from God. But being in a different place (like far from home) is not the same as going against what God says is right (like being with someone else's wife). One is about location, the other is about doing what's right or wrong.

God always knows where we are geographically as well as morally. Distance and darkness never blind God to our moral hiding place. His omniscience is not limited to our street address. We should always remember the name by which Hagar called God, "You are the God who sees me" (Gen 16:13).

RIGHT ON THE MONEY

Have you ever taken a good look at our currency? Every coin and bill has stamped on it, IN GOD WE TRUST. This is ironic because Proverbs 11:28 tells us that whoever trusts in riches will fail. Think about this for a moment. The very thing God tells us to trust in the least (money) has written on it the very One we are to trust in the most (God). Strangely enough, we tend to trust more in the former than the latter.

Money does strange things to all of us. There is an interesting word that seems only to be used in the context of wealth. That word is *independently*. We never say someone is independently athletic or independently good-looking, but we do say they are independently wealthy. Really? Does that mean that if I have a billion dollars, I am no longer dependent on God? Can money bring my prodigal home, restore my troubled marriage, or buy my way out of a terminal illness? Other terms, such as financial security, carry the same weight as declaring our independence. Wealth often creates an illusion of control and security, convincing us that we can manage every aspect of our lives. But then the day comes when the rug is pulled out from under our financial feet, and we are in free fall. Though we are independently wealthy, we can't buy our way out of the mess.

When this reality hits, the word *hopelessly* replaces the word *independently*. So, pull a bill out of your wallet or purse and stare at the bold statement IN GOD WE TRUST. Jesus said, "Where your treasure is, there your heart will be also" (Mat 6:21). We just might find that we are more dependent than we thought. Proverbs 23:5 says money has wings and flies away. So, I guess the old adage that "money talks" is true. It says, "Goodbye!"

CONFESSIONS OF AN ATHEIST

I suspect that some of you wrestle with the existence of God, and maybe those of you who believe He exists have trouble explaining to yourself why you believe.

If God does not exist, then we are nothing more than a collection of chemicals stimulated by electrical signals. You could say, for the sake of example, that we are nothing more than bags of fertilizer. At last count, there are about eight billion bags on this globe. It clearly means that our lives lack any inherent purpose or meaning beyond mere survival. This will lead to a sense of existential emptiness or nihilism, where life is reduced to biological processes without deeper significance.

If you don't believe in God and someone steals your car, you get angry with the thief. Yet he can always plead innocence by saying that his chemicals told him to steal your car, and your chemicals told you to get mad at the injustice.

If you don't believe in God and your spouse cheats on you, you get angry. But, like the thief, your spouse can plead innocence since his or her electrical signals told them to cheat, and yours told you to get mad.

Here are two non-believers getting upset by a violation of two of the Ten Commandments—stealing and adultery. And what could the offended spouse really say if the offending spouse asked, "Are you trying to impose your moral values on me, you self-righteous prude?"

So why don't we stop arguing over the existence of God and get on with our lives and chalk up our differences to chemistry? Because everyone's chemistry seems to know right from wrong, and our chemistry seems to affirm a moral law, which implies an intelligence behind this law. So, unbelievers and believers share a common ancestor. Scripture declares that we are all the offspring of God.

I suspect an atheist could argue that he follows these laws because it is best for society and his personal life. But what would make him argue this point other than chemistry and electricity? And what does he mean when he tells his ten-year-old daughter that he loves her? "Oh, Dad, that's just your chemistry speaking." But, then again, that would be her chemistry speaking as well. Intimacy replaced by chemistry. NO THANKS.

CALCULATING THE AVERAGE

A six-year-old boy goes to his friend's birthday party. The host parents have the little guys go into the backyard and play baseball with a plastic bat and ball. The first little guy steps up and swings, but well after the ball has crossed the imaginary plate. A second boy steps up and manages to hit the ball about ten feet. A third boy steps up and cracks the ball over the roof.

The first kid realizes he is below average and will never put himself in this humiliating spot again. The second realizes he is above average and figures he won't get laughed at too much. The third kid thinks he is a lot better than average and can already smell a Major League contract. All three are calculating the average, even though they have no idea what "calculate" or "average" means. Such calculations start around age six and don't stop until the grave.

We calculate the average every day. We know where we stand athletically, academically, physically, and socially. That's because the world we live in sets unrealistic standards, and if we don't meet them, people look down on us. Much unhappiness and despair are born from calculating the average.

However, once we become secure in Christ, these false and humiliating standards begin to fade, for there is no average in the Kingdom of God. But this process will not happen overnight. It must be a truth in which your soul marinates. The only standard you will be measured by is the perfect standard of God's righteousness.

Talk about calculating the average. Thank God this perfection is given to us as a gift when we put our faith in Jesus Christ.

So, rest easy. In His calculation, we have been declared righteous, and that's a home run with the bases loaded.

IS ALL SIN THE SAME?

Have you ever heard someone say that all sin is the same? In one sense, that is true, but in another, it's false. For instance, if you have not put your faith in Christ, then all sin is the same for this reason: One sin or ten million sins will keep you out of heaven because God cannot allow any sin into His perfect home. If, on the other hand, you are a follower of Christ, then all sin is not the same. I Corinthians 6:18-20 explains, for example, that sexual sin is especially serious because it's a sin against one's body, which is the temple of the Holy Spirit. Lying to your spouse about what you spent at the mall will have a very different consequence than lying to cover up an affair.

Sometimes, the reason people say that all sins are the same is that it gives them an excuse to live as they please. When confronted by a friend that their adultery is a serious matter, they may respond with, "You speed, and I commit adultery; all sin is the same."

Another way to excuse sin is by quoting the Apostle Paul when he said, "You are not under the law, but under grace" (Rom 6:14). Does this mean I can live as I please? By no means. Not being under the law simply means the law can no longer condemn me because God's grace has forgiven me. Paul never meant that the law is not to be obeyed, for the law is holy and just and good (Rom 7:12).

On the contrary, the law is to be obeyed, but not in order to earn one's salvation. That is where grace comes in. Grace empowers us to live a life pleasing to God, not an excuse to live our lives as we please. You can see how convenient such justification is for violating God's law.

We all need to take a careful inventory of our lives and see if we are looking for loopholes to avoid living a life that is pleasing to God.

LIFE WILL BE BETTER WHEN...

How many times have we said to ourselves that "life will be better when...?" You supply the *when*. Life will be better when I get my driver's license. Life will be better when I graduate from college, when I get married, when we have children, or when I am making more money. The truth is that you are presently experiencing many of the *whens* that you thought were going to make life a lot better. But time tells a different story. Now, there is a new set of *whens*. Life will be better when I achieve that dream job. Life will be better when I finally retire and have all the free time I desire. Age seems to dictate what *whens* we idolize the most. When we were young, we idolized the privileges that come with age, such as a home, a car, and a nice income. When we are older, we idolize the privileges of youth, like teeth, memory, and a full head of hair. Future *whens* and past *whens* never seem to leave us alone.

Could it be that the *whens* of life just might be a mirage? Will any of them ever fulfill what can only be fulfilled when we stop idolizing about the next when? *Whens* are temporary fixes. They are fillers. This is patchwork at its best. It seems to be deeply entrenched in the human soul to always look for the fountain of youth or the pot of gold at the end of the rainbow. We all desire to be redeemed, but only Christ can offer this.

So, take an inventory of your *whens*. See how many of them are temporal. See how many of them you can take with you when you pass from this world. See how many fall into the category of "Don't store up for yourselves treasures on earth, where moth and rust destroy and where thieves break in and steal" (Mat 6:19, CSB). As the old hymn by Esther K. Rusthoi says, "It will be worth it all when we see Jesus," which is the only *when* that counts.

MIDLIFE CRISIS

Genesis tells us that Methuselah lived to be 969 years old. You can't help but wonder if he had a midlife crisis. A midlife crisis happens when you realize there is more sand at the bottom of the hourglass than at the top. It's panic time. This realization often leads to reflection on unfulfilled dreams and missed opportunities, prompting many to reassess their life choices and priorities. Additionally, as individuals confront their own mortality, they may feel a sense of urgency to make significant changes, whether that's pursuing a long-lost passion, switching careers, or rekindling relationships that have faded over time.

Was Methuselah plagued by the fact that time was running out? Did he say to his wife, "Martha, where have the centuries gone? Why, it seems like just yesterday that we celebrated my 300th birthday, and now look at me at 500. Gray hair is starting to set in. I see some new wrinkles under my eyes." I doubt this conversation took place, but if he lived in our day and age, it probably would have.

Let's ponder this midlife crisis phenomenon. If Methuselah lived 969 years and someone else lives to be only twenty, is there really any difference, since Scripture tells us that life is a vapor (Jam 4:14)? Doesn't that compelling truth relate to all of us, no matter our longevity in this world?

Here is something else to think about. Jesus said, "Very truly I tell you, the one who believes has eternal life" (John 6:47). If my life is everlasting, then how can I have a midlife crisis? Where is the midpoint in a life that never ends? Perhaps this whole midlife issue is an invention of our materialistic culture that believes the old adage that says, "You only go around once in life, so grab for all the gusto you can!"

The Apostle Paul gives us the remedy when he says, "Set your minds on things above, not on earthly things" (Col 3:2). To have a midlife crisis assumes you are at the midpoint when you may be closer to the end than you think. Rejoice in the fact that everlasting life begins the moment you put your trust in Christ, and there is no midpoint in eternity.

AN INTOLERANT GRACE

I suspect that most of us have heard about the parable of the prodigal son (Luke 15:11-32). Even if you don't consider yourself a follower of Jesus, you might use the expression "prodigal" if you have a wayward child. Let's review the parable for a moment. The younger son goes to his father (who represents God in the parable) and asks for an early inheritance. He runs off to a far country and spends his wealth on wild living. He soon comes to his senses and decides to return home. As he returns, the son rehearses what he is going to say to his father (vv. 18-19).

Point 1: "Father, I have sinned against heaven."

Point 2: "And against you."

Point 3: "I am no longer worthy to be called your son."

Point 4: "Make me like one of your hired men."

It's interesting to note that when he delivers the message to his father, his father only allows him to say three out of his four points before stopping him mid-sentence. He never gets to say, "Make me one of your hired men." Why doesn't the father allow him to finish? Because "make me one of your hired men" is an attempt to earn his father's love.

God accepts us by His grace, not by our performance. Grace is not granted based on performance (Gal 2:21). The son feels that if he grovels enough and works hard enough, his father will accept him. Since his father represents God, we learn that we can never do enough to earn a place at His table. That is why salvation is all by grace and not by any amount of good works. So, stop the performance. He is not impressed. Instead, rejoice in His amazing grace that saves us, keeps us, and teaches us.

IT MAY NOT SUIT YOU

Many are familiar with the account of David and Goliath (1 Sam 17). Saul was king of Israel at the time of this conflict, and he felt David needed to be properly prepared, so he lent David his armor. David tried it on but felt uncomfortable and went to battle with a slingshot.

Why does God tell us that David took off Saul's armor? Perhaps the armor would have gotten the glory and not God, but I don't think this is the real reason.

All of us who profess Christ tend to put on another person's armor. We hear a testimony of how someone applied three biblical principles that restored their marriage, so we try that, and it doesn't work. We hear how someone prayed a certain prayer and got healed, so we try the prayer, but the illness fails to go away.

What is happening is we are trying on someone else's armor. We think the armor is a formula, but there are no formulas. The armor God gives one of His children is custom-fit for them and their pilgrimage in this world. Testimonies are not formulas.

We discover that once David took off Saul's armor, he then took *his* staff, *his* sling, and some stones he gathered in *his* bag (1 Sam 17:40). Note the emphasis on *his*, not Saul's. Other people's testimonies are not transferable and should not be copied. They are personal accounts of how God has uniquely given armor to His people for certain situations, so let's not try to carry someone else's sword in our scabbard.

You have your own slingshot that will be given to you when needed, but it will not be given until you take off the borrowed armor of another's experience. Another person's sword does not slay your giants, but the one personally crafted by the Lord for your battle. So, when the battle comes, you will be given your own armor, and it will suit you well.

AN UNLIKELY FRIENDSHIP

The subject of law and grace has always been a sticky issue in the world of the church. We love to quote verses that lend support to our view on this subject.

Some feel that going to heaven is based on how well they keep the commandments, though few people can even name them. Our natural tendency is to think the law can save us. This most likely comes from the fact that life rewards those who try hard and keep the rules—we best try to keep the law since this is our ticket into the Kingdom. But others quote the Apostle Paul, who said, "…you are not under the law, but under grace" (Rom 6:14b).

Let's see if we can get law and grace to shake hands. Law and grace become enemies if we emphasize one over the other. But law and grace become friends when they are reconciled in the Gospel. Why is that? I remind myself of this: I have a right relationship with the law and a right relationship with grace because I have a right relationship with Christ, who lovingly kept the law for me and graciously placed to my account all the perfection the law demands.

The law reveals God's righteous standard, yet my human effort can never reach it. Grace, on the other hand, fulfills the demands of the law. How do I know this? Because Jesus said, "Do not think that I have come to abolish the Law or the Prophets; I have not come to abolish them but to fulfill them" (Mat 5:17). Just think how freeing that is. I can't possibly keep the demands of the law, so Jesus did it for me, and now the law can no longer condemn me. Is that good news or what? But remember, law and grace only shake hands if you know Jesus as the one who rescued us from living under the curse of the law and graciously forgave us. Only in Christ do law and grace embrace.

WHAT WAS I THINKING?

There is a question we often ask ourselves that borders on lunacy. It usually falls from our lips right after we have done something really stupid. It is often asked with great emotion, but a little late. When our poor decision comes to light, "What was I thinking?" is shouted from the housetops. We simply can't believe we made such a foolish investment or left the stove on all day. In those moments, we grapple with feelings of regret and embarrassment, wishing we could turn back time and make a different choice.

However, those don't usually ruin our lives. But what about the biggies? You know, the ones we read about in the paper when a high-ranking military officer gets entangled in an affair or a member of Congress gets money under the table for pushing a contract that benefits one company over another. We read about jail time or an ensuing divorce.

This is not minor stuff—we are talking about a whole life falling into ruin, not to mention all those in the fallout zone. The guilty parties lie awake at night, taking inventory of the foolish behavior that ushered them into this black hole. "What was I thinking?" is the cry from their hearts. They wish they could rewind the tape, but wishful thinking cannot repair the damage. Most people act spontaneously in a situation without thinking. As believers, we must heed the warning from the Apostle Paul when he said, "We take captive every thought to make it obedient to Christ" (2 Cor 10:5b).

There is a far better question when temptation comes knocking: "What *am* I thinking?" Now, we can put on the brakes. Contemplating an affair, cheating a customer, or lying to your employer? Remember, "What *am* I thinking?" is a far better question than later having to ask "What *was* I thinking?". By taking a moment to reflect on our actions and their potential consequences, we gain clarity and can make more informed choices. Think about it.

MOLEHILLS OUT OF MOUNTAINS

We have all heard the expression "making mountains out of molehills." But have we ever considered that sometimes we make molehills out of mountains? In other words, we play down what is big in the eyes of God.

This is perhaps seen most in the world of entertainment. "Okay, so the movie had a few sex scenes. What's the big deal? It is part of our culture." The real question that begs to be answered is, "Since when does culture determine my moral values?" There will always be a slow drift in culture to move away from a divine standard. Video games, reality TV, entertainment magazines, and a host of other media outlets give us instant access to the devil's playground. The normalization of such content can desensitize us, making it harder to recognize right from wrong. It's crucial to critically evaluate what we consume and ensure it aligns with our core beliefs.

It used to be that if you wanted to see something morally debased, you needed to go to the raunchy side of town and slip into a back-alley theater with your collar flipped up and your head down lest anyone see you. Now, we willingly drop the kids off to see things that once were considered adult entertainment by the world.

What's happened? We have made molehills out of mountains. God considers sexual matters of the gravest importance. These are the moral Mount Everests we face daily.

The Psalmist says, "I will set no wicked thing before mine eyes" (Ps 101:3, KJV). The Apostle Paul reminds us to "flee the evil desires of youth" (2 Tim 2:22). How much of what we watch or look at would we stop taking in if we truly obeyed these two verses?

Sexual immorality may not be a mountain you view as a molehill. A host of others have been reduced to the size of a pitcher's mound: greed, materialism, injustice, forsaking the poor, etc. Just remember this: moles live in the dark, and so do we when we make molehills out of mountains.

REMEMBER TO FORGET

Have you ever come to a red light and the person in front of you is fiddling with their cell phone? The light turns green, but they are immersed in texting. You begin to fume, give a slight tap on your horn, and mumble under your breath, "What a self-centered jerk." The next day, you're at the same light, but the scene is reversed. You're the one texting when the light turns green, and you hear a slight honk from the car behind you. You mumble under your breath, "What an impatient jerk." Strange, isn't it, how we view ourselves? In one respect, we could be called selfish. In another, we could be called a hypocrite. I guess this is why Scripture says, "The heart is deceitful above all things, and desperately wicked; who can know it?" (Jer 17:9).

This same heart disease bubbles up in other arenas. If someone in authority, like a boss or parent, does something nice for you, it fails to make it in your memory bank, but if they do it for a coworker or sibling, you suddenly have an accurate accounting system that will later be leveraged to say they are showing favoritism. This is why we vividly recall all the instances our dad took our brother fishing, yet we struggle to remember the times he attended our football games.

When the Israelites were in the desert, they forgot the slavery in Egypt, but remembered the food. Memory has a habit of being very selective. Depending on what favors me most, I will remember to forget or forget to remember. Memory plays favorites. Memory is prejudiced, and it always sides with me. I am my memory's favorite person.

Well, I had better bring this to a close because the guy in front of me is not moving, and the light is green. But then again, maybe it's an emergency phone call, and the light can wait. You never know.

LOOKING BEYOND THE PROMISE

The Bible is a book of tension. Certain truths seemingly pull against each other. It's a little like tug of war. We have God's sovereignty on one end and a person's moral responsibility on the other. This can create tension for us when reading Scripture.

Here's a tension to ponder. Abraham is told that he is going to have a son and that all the world will be blessed through his offspring. But when Isaac arrives, God tells Abraham to offer up his son. So, what we have is God's promise of a son being challenged by His command to destroy the promise. His promise and command collide. What's up with that? And is there a resolution?

Abraham struggled to trust God from time to time. However, near the end of his life, he was faced with the biggest challenge of all—killing his own son. What must have been going through his mind as he pondered God's command that challenged God's promise? We don't have to wonder! The New Testament tells us that he believed that God could raise his son from the dead (Heb 11:19). In other words, Abraham had to look beyond the promise to see that God would fulfill His promise in a greater way than the human mind could conceive: resurrection. Many of God's promises are not going to be fulfilled in this world, which is why it is said of the great saints, "All these people were still living by faith when they died. They did not receive the things promised; they only saw them and welcomed them from a distance, admitting that they were foreigners and strangers on earth" (Heb 11:13). So, take a long look through the lens of Scripture and focus on that which is eternal. It makes His promises come alive.

LEARNING THE WORD

The Bible gives us many tools to help us understand its message, but I want to focus on four.

The first of the disciplines is simply to read it (Matt 19:4). We ought to do this daily. The Bible is like a guide walking us through the forest that is our life. As we follow its lead, it helps us become familiar with our world, ourselves, and most importantly, God Himself.

The second is to study the word, which is like observing the forest and noting the many varieties of life that inhabit its terrain (2 Tim 2:15). Studying helps us move from mere knowledge to understanding and application.

The third is to memorize the Scriptures, which is equivalent to being able to identify the leaves or animals in the forest from memory. Memorization helps us recall what the word says in times of need. It helps us walk according to its ways (Ps 119:1).

The fourth is to meditate (or reflect) on the word, which is to experience the beauty and essence of the forest. It's like taking a hike and then sitting quietly and waiting for life to manifest itself (Ps 1:1-3).

This last discipline, meditation, is the one most often overlooked. Yet there is a promise attached to it. Those who meditate day and night will prosper in this life. Biblical prosperity is living victoriously in all the ways God values. One way to think about the difference between studying the word and meditating on it is this: our intellect examines the essence of Scripture while our meditation transforms it into sustenance. This is why David said in the Psalms, "Open my eyes that I may see wonderful things in your law" (Ps 119:18).

It is quite clear that there are deeper truths only found beneath the surface of God's Word. We must mine for them. So, find a quiet place, and let the word saturate your mind. What the Lord teaches you will never be a new doctrine, nor will it ever contradict any truth in Scripture, but it will speak personally to you as His child and breathe new life into your spirit. Meditation is the mother of insight.

ENCOURAGEMENT

Here are a few tips on why and how we need to encourage and be encouraged:

1. We all need to be stroked by the warm hand of encouragement because, through much tribulation, we enter into the Kingdom of God (Acts 14:22).
2. Encouragement develops friendships. We naturally seek out those who refresh us with words of comfort and avoid those who destroy us with words of criticism. It gives health to the recipient. Proverbs 16:24 tells us that "Gracious words are a honeycomb, sweet to the soul and healing to the bones."
3. We hurt far more deeply than we will admit. Most people carry burdens the weight of which an outsider cannot estimate.
4. Learn to encourage when you sense a need.
5. Learn to relate to those who have similar needs. Be mindful and compassionate toward those facing challenges similar to those you've already endured. How did you weather the storm? Let them know how God used that difficulty in your life.
6. Learn to be a good listener.
7. No one will expose their deeper feelings to people who show little or no interest. Be a person who cares!

Our emotional balance sheet reveals that we tend to receive much more criticism than praise. So, who do you know who needs some encouragement right now? Reach out and lift up their spirits while we wait for Christ's coming (Heb 10:24-25).

AN ARM'S LENGTH

Sometimes we feel safe by telling ourselves that staying a few steps behind the world is a wise way to live. The problem is that as society continues to move farther away from God, so do we, if we only maintain a few steps behind. The world always moves in a direction that is in opposition to God's standard. So, to keep an arm's length means we are just a few paces behind its values and morality.

This type of thinking leads us to the logical conclusion that if we keep this pace, then tomorrow we will be living by the world's standards of today. Many of us are now engaging with things we would have opposed in the past. Think about the movie "Gone With The Wind." In it, Clark Gable used the word "damn." The world was shocked. Today, many believers barely even notice such language anymore. We've grown accustomed to it. As an old preacher once said, "We've gotten used to the dark."

The Apostle Paul said, "May I never boast except in the cross of our Lord Jesus Christ, through which the world has been crucified to me, and I to the world" (Gal 6:14). Meaning, I am dead to the world, and it is dead to me. It is better to keep our backs to the world so it can follow us than to keep an arm's length from the world so we can follow it.

CONTENTMENT

We are constantly being told what we need in life in order to be content. The barrage of commercials will never let us forget how much better life would be if we just had the latest car, iPad, medication, etc.

Have you ever noticed that kingdom living, as found in Scripture, seems to go against the grain of how the world thinks? Consider the following reversals. Kingdom living tells us we are to give in order to get (Lk 6:38). We are to be humble in order to be lifted up (1 Pet 5:6). We are to die in order to live (Lk 17:33). We are to love our enemies, not hate them (Mat 5:44). We are to serve in order to lead (Mat 23:11). None of this feels right, nor does it come naturally.

Biblical contentment is coming to a place in my life where I desire nothing as opposed to needing to have everything. The Apostle Paul said that in whatever state he found himself, he learned to be content (Phil 4:11). He was content when he had plenty and content when he had little. He explained that he had to learn this kind of contentment. By nature, we are not content. Contentment is a virtue that must be cultivated. Perhaps the best way to do this is to look around at what we presently own and see if it has brought the contentment we hoped for. Most likely, it has not. Yet we keep piling it on. The definition of insanity is doing the same thing over and over and hoping for different results. So, let's come to our senses and get rid of the clutter. We just might find the peace we have been looking for buried under the pile.

FEAR

Scripture tells us that the fear of others brings a snare (Prov 29:25). Fearing others may mean we don't like to confront because we're afraid of retaliation or losing someone as a friend. Some, on the other hand, have no problem confronting others, citing their lack of fear. But these are often driven types of people who are success-oriented. They fear the task or goal will not be accomplished, and others will not see them as successful. This is just another form of fear.

So, we have two types of fear—the fear of not being liked and the fear of not being seen as successful. These are simply two sides of the same coin. It's time to take stock and figure out which of these fears is really running the show in our lives.

Being afraid that people won't like me is a type of idolatry. Being afraid of not being seen as successful is another form of idolatry. Idolatry tends to dictate how we live.

God tells us over and over to worship Him and Him alone (Exod 20:3; Isa 42:8). At first blush, it appears as though God has a self-image problem. But the truth is that God knows that if we don't worship Him, then we will worship something else. And He knows that anything else leads to emptiness. Worship is our awareness of and reverent response to God's presence in our lives.

So, it's not a self-image problem on God's part but an idolatry problem on ours. This is why worship is so important. It keeps God first in our lives and keeps idols where they belong—nonexistent.

WHO ARE "THEY"?

They say you shouldn't go swimming after eating. They say caffeine is bad for you. They say too much sun increases aging. The question I have is: Who are "they"?

I think "they" is an imaginary group of people who come to our rescue when we want to prove a point or win an argument. We recruit this phantom group more than we want to admit. Whenever we want to prove we are right, "they" come alongside and win the day. It's fine when it comes to trivial things, like when "they" say the stock market might dip this week or "they" predict the Yankees could win the World Series.

But what about eternal matters? "They" say good people go to heaven and bad people go to hell. Again, such statements beg the question: Who are "they"? Eternal matters are big issues, and I don't want the opinion of "they" but "He"—that is, God Himself. I need to know what He says, which will always trump what "they" say. I don't want to take any chances on my eternal destiny based on the imaginary "they."

"They" may represent a large block of people. Religion, atheism, and a host of worldviews all have their favorite group of "they" who have all the answers. But He says my entrance into heaven has nothing to do with my goodness and everything to do with His gift. Eternal life is a gift given to those who put their faith in Christ alone. So, in the end, "their" opinion is bankrupt, while His opinion is treasured forevermore.

THAT'S NOT FAIR

We often say, "That's not fair." The truth is that life is not fair, and it never will be. Asaph, who wrote Psalm 73, complained in the first half of the Psalm that wicked people prosper and the rest of us who sacrifice for the Lord spend our days being overlooked and neglected by God. We must separate out how God views fairness and justice and how humanity sees them. When we confuse the two, life gets messy. God doesn't talk about fairness but justice. You see, fairness is measured on a temporal scale, while God's justice is measured on an eternal scale. This is a valuable lesson to learn early in life because it keeps us from being frustrated with all the favoritism shown to others when we get left out. It shows why life seems to go well for many who have no interest in God and treat believers so poorly at times.

Asaph really struggled with this and became depressed. That is, until he went into the sanctuary of the Lord. His eyes were opened to the competing issues of fairness and justice. God revealed to him that he would one day be taken to glory while those outside the Kingdom would find themselves suddenly consumed with terror.

Life is not fair—but it is just. So, the next time you break a cookie in half and give one half to one child and the other half to another child, watch carefully what they do. They immediately eye each other's cookies to see whose is bigger. The child with the smaller piece will cry, "It's not fair," to which you can now respond, "Life is not fair, but God is just." I'm not sure they will buy it, but it's worth a try!

PRAYER

Prayer has always been a mystery to me. I find Bible study and meditation (pondering or reflecting on Scripture) easy, but I find prayer to be the hardest discipline in the Christian life. Here are some reasons why I think this is so. If we pray and it is not answered the way we felt it should be, then we are disappointed. We become fearful of prayer lest we get burned by disappointment again. Answers are rarely immediate, and when answered, we often can't detect the connection between the request and the answer.

Sometimes, our prayers are self-centered. They are all about us rather than the glory of God. Praying prayers of worship and adoration requires putting God first above our own selves. Prayer also requires concentration when our minds tend to wander off in many directions. Even when we become determined to stay focused, our prayer sounds something like, "Lord, thank You for today and the good weather that we have experienced. I wonder how the weather works? All those puffy clouds look like scoops of ice cream. I think ice cream is on sale this week. If I am not mistaken, you buy one and get the other for half price." Yes, such wandering off into Neverland happens more often than we want to admit.

I believe our prayers fall short because we're not comfortable talking to a stranger. The deeper our relationship with God, the richer our prayer life becomes, just like any close friendship. Is God a stranger? Is He a distant relative that we rarely speak to? Or can we truly say, "Our Father in heaven…" (Mat 6:9, KJV)?

IF I LIVED BY THE GOLDEN RULE

If I truly lived by the Golden Rule, I'd never make it through the day. I'd probably never even get to work, constantly stopping to help others the way I'd hoped they'd help me. I could not make enough hospital visits or bake enough food to meet every need of the poor. So, let's all agree that none of us lives by the Golden Rule. So why does the Lord tell us to conduct our lives this way? Have you ever noticed that the Lord never says, "To the best of your ability, pray when you get a chance"? Instead, He says, "pray continually" (1 Thes 5:17). He doesn't say, "Meditate if there is time in your schedule," but rather, "Meditate on it day and night" (Ps 1:1-3). The Lord doesn't say, "Try your best," but rather, "Be perfect, therefore, as your heavenly Father is perfect" (Mat 5:48), or "Be holy, because I am holy" (1 Pet 1:16).

God's standard could never be anything but perfection. Thus, the Golden Rule. This is the heart of the Gospel: Christ lived out what I couldn't. He didn't have to meditate day and night because He is the living word. He is the answer to prayer. He is the embodiment of the Golden Rule. So, to be in Christ is to have carried out all of these impossible demands. 2 Corinthians 5:21 tells us that we have become the righteousness of God in Christ. The righteousness that we could not achieve on our own, He achieved for us.

Should we now decide never to pray? Should we forget to live by the Golden Rule? To quote the Apostle Paul, "By no means" (Rom 6:2). This is now our motivation: the power of the Gospel. "The life I now live in the body, I live by faith in the Son of God, who loved me and gave himself for me" (Gal 2:20).

HONESTY VS. INTEGRITY

If I were honest, then I would have to admit that I'm not all that honest, for Scripture makes a proper assessment of my heart when it says, "Let God be true, and every human being a liar" (Rom 3:4). However, Scripture also tells us of honest people who are upright and have integrity, such as Job and Daniel. So, which is it? If God is the measuring stick, then the assessment in Scripture is correct, but if man is the measuring stick, then certain people can be referred to as honest with respect to others. Rationalization, however, will keep me focused on the latter rather than the former.

If I am honest, I will allow Scripture to keep these two in proper balance. If I put too much weight on one side of the scale, then I will become self-absorbed and overly introspective about my sins. If I put too much weight on the other side, then I become self-exalting, "God, I thank you that I am not like other people..." (Lk 18:11).

So, how am I to see my honesty? Let's first admit that it is quite possible to be honest while at the same time lacking integrity. How can this be? Because we can compartmentalize our honesty but not our integrity. Integrity deals with the whole person. The word "integrity" comes from the same source as the word "integer," which means a whole number. A man can be meticulously honest in filling out his income tax while at the same time cheating on his wife. His honesty is compartmentalized. He is honest in one area but lacks integrity as a whole.

In all honesty, I would recognize the importance of being a person of integrity. Otherwise, I would rationalize and think I am honest just because I don't cheat on my income tax, and April 15 is always just around the corner.

FORGIVEN LEADS TO FORGIVENESS

If I truly embraced forgiveness, it would reflect my understanding of Christ's grace. Yet, the power of rationalization is an unyielding force. You see, God can forgive because He is perfect; however, I am not. How then can I be expected to forgive when I lack such perfection? Not to mention, we tend to rationalize: What others have done to me is worse than anything I have done to God, so obviously, God can forgive me more readily than I can forgive others. Right? However, if I were forgiving, I would have to take this line of reasoning to its logical conclusion and realize that those I have offended believe that what I have done to them is worse than anything they have done to God. This will always result in a stalemate.

If I were forgiving, I would not make comparisons about the degree of wrongdoing but focus on the Cross, where all forgiveness must be sought. There is a level playing field at Calvary. In the midst of my pain, I would return to this hill and ask God to search me and see if there is any wicked way in me (Psalm 139:23-34).

If I were truly forgiving, I wouldn't get caught up in the numbers game of assigning blame percentages. Rationalization is tough to shake off, and you could argue that the situation you're struggling to let go of isn't really about percentages at all. They slandered your reputation without being provoked, which puts all the blame squarely on their shoulders. Calvary comes into view again. Jesus did nothing wrong, yet took all the blame. "When they hurled their insults at him, he did not retaliate; when he suffered, he made no threats. Instead, he entrusted himself to him who judges justly" (1 Pet 2:23).

Is there not a message here? The Cross forgives even my unforgiveness (Col 3:13). None of us has ever forgiven perfectly, but our Substitute has. Jesus has not only forgiven all who come to Him but has taught us how to forgive those who have hurt us the most. True forgiveness is costly because I give up my right to get even.

ARE YOU TEACHABLE?

When someone approaches us with criticism, rationalization is sure to find its way into the discussion. Criticism puts our internal defenses on high alert: "But what they said was not completely true!" "What they said was not communicated in a kind manner!" But so, what? The question on the table is not the degree of truth in the criticism or even how it was delivered, but whether there is something for me to learn from it. Am I teachable? After all, God was not taken by surprise by what was said or how it was delivered. He knew this criticism was part of conforming you to His image. Could it be that He has something for you to learn through it?

When pride kicks in, we might become defensive and claim that a half-truth is just a lie, making any criticism aimed at us seem unjustified. Not so fast. Half-truths are invalid in the world of objective reality, but not subjective reality. A half-truth about what a product can deliver can easily be dismissed as a lie. However, a half-truth about your character is a different story—one that deserves a bit more thought. Thus, the question, "Am I teachable?"

If I were open to learning, I would sort through everything said about me to find any truth in it. If I were teachable, I might seek out a good friend and run the criticism by them to see if there is any truth in it. I really dislike coming home after hanging out with friends only to discover I had spinach stuck between my teeth the whole time. Why didn't someone say something? Sporting spinach is a far cry from sporting bad character. Tell me, please! I want to know, even if it is not said in a kind fashion.

So, if I am teachable, then I will seek the counsel of the most teachable One of all, of whom it was said, "He learned obedience from what He suffered" (Heb 5:8). We will suffer in learning to be teachable, but we will be far more Christ-like when the lesson is learned.

THE ULTIMATE DELIGHT

If I delight in the Lord, then according to Psalm 37:4, I will be given the desires of my heart. We consider this to be a blank check, and whatever we ask will be given if we delight in the Lord. But let's analyze this for a moment. I want a new Rolls-Royce, and since I am delighting in the Lord, He will give it to me. Really? Since when does someone delighting in the Lord want a Rolls? Their delight is in stuff and not the Lord. "Do not love the world or anything in the world" (1 Jn 2:15).

There is another, more sensitive way to look at this verse. "I really want children" or "I really desire to be married" is the cry of many who have delighted in the Lord, yet their desires remain unfulfilled. But these are normal desires of all humans and not just believers.

A third understanding of the verse is that God places strong desires on our hearts when we delight in Him that cannot be fulfilled in any other way but by supernatural grace. So, if I am delighting in the Lord, then I might expect that He will give me an overwhelming desire to advance the Kingdom in ways that are beyond my normal desires and capabilities. A missionary call or a deep desire to start a Bible study at work may well fall into this category. "The one who calls you is faithful, and He will do it" (1 Thes 5:24).

When I find joy in the Lord, I can look forward to Him acting in ways that bring Him joy. These moments are thrilling and defy any human explanation. And by the way, there is nothing wrong with a Rolls-Royce. Just don't drive it to church because the pastor may ask whether or not you tithe.

THE EYES OF FAITH

If I walked by faith and not by sight, then my faith would be the glasses for my sight. My eyes would look through the lens of faith. Faith would determine what I really see. My eyes would see, but my faith would interpret. When I walk by faith instead of by sight, my faith acts like spiritual eyes, enabling me to see beyond my immediate surroundings. I need my eyes to guide me through this physical world and my faith to see the world as God sees it. My human senses are not bad. They are gifts from God designed to help us navigate this world, but they don't always provide the best insights into the deeper issues of life.

When it is said of Abraham in Hebrews 11:10 that he was looking forward to a heavenly city built by God, the passage is not referring to Abraham's eyes but to his faith in what God had promised. Jesus also referred to this great man of faith when He said, "Your father Abraham rejoiced at the thought of seeing my day; he saw it and was glad" (Jn 8:56). It is said of Moses in Hebrews that "he saw him who is invisible" (Heb 11:27).

Faith doesn't dismiss or replace our human abilities; it simply extends beyond what we can sense. My human wisdom might show me my bank balance, but my faith reminds me not to rely solely on it. My human wisdom can tell me how smart I am, but my faith tells me that I have the mind of Christ. My human wisdom can tell me how healthy I am, but my faith tells me that I will live forever. Faith leads me to trust God's Word even when it makes no human sense to do so. Spiritual eyes see well beyond physical eyes, which is why we are told not to be wise in our own eyes but to fear the Lord and depart from evil (Prov 3:7).

PREJUDICE AGAINST BIAS

If I were unbiased, then I would be able to make proper judgments in life without any thought of personal gain. My own desired results would not color a predetermined outcome. If I were truly unbiased, I would base my decisions on what is actually true, not just on what I wish were true. I'd view every situation requiring a choice without being swayed by personality, relationships, personal gain, political views, or even my life in America.

Reality says, "Let's get serious. Who could possibly live under such constraints?" No doubt, being unbiased will be a threat to our character as long as we live.

If I were unbiased, I would want to make sure I don't use excuses for my personal prejudices but weigh all matters on the scales of biblical justice. If I love hymns, I may become biased to the point that any songs written in the past twenty years must be shallow and lack doctrinal content. If I'm a fan of praise songs, I might become so biased that I view anything written before this century as stuffy, dull, and unexciting. If Scripture is silent on such issues, then preference may rule out what I like—but it should never rule out what I don't like. (This assumes the old and the new are biblically sound.)

Do I ever find myself interpreting Scripture through the lens of my favorite theological system rather than letting Scripture speak for itself? This may cause me to miss what God is saying to me, or worse, to tell Him what He should be saying to me rather than what He is saying to me. Bias often overrules my integrity when integrity should always overrule my bias.

HOW TO RECEIVE CORRECTIONS

Giving correction is one thing, but receiving it is another. Proverbs has much to say about how a wise person becomes even wiser after correction and how a fool despises any type of rebuke (Prov 1:7; 9:9). None of us wants to be labeled by Scripture as a fool, but few people receive good correction well. So, what does God tell us?

Don't be defensive. Remember, the person approaching us might have valuable advice that could improve our careers, home life, and other relationships. Always view correction as protection. Even if the person who performs the surgery fails to do it skillfully, it may still benefit you in the long run.

Understand that your self-perception differs from how others see you. We often have an inflated view of how we present ourselves, which influences how we interact with others. Those who are around us most feel the radiation of our personality that we don't experience ourselves because the source of radiation is directed outward. This is why we need honest feedback from those who love us. Don't expect people to correct you in a godly manner. Most people, including many believers, are unaware of how to do this. Instead, when you are corrected, consider the following:

1. What was said? Ponder any truth that comes with the correction.
2. Who said it? The amount of truth is directly proportional to the credibility of the one who said it.
3. Let them say it. You can dig through and remove the bones later. Teachability is humility in action.

PILGRIMS

King David said in Psalm 119:19 that he was a stranger in the earth. Who would use such language except a foreigner? He didn't say he was a stranger in Israel or France, but on Earth. To use such an expression clearly means he is from another place.

If I, as a North American, were in Germany and asked for directions from a native German, I might begin by saying that I am a stranger in his land. This would obviously mean that I am from another country. The same could be said when traveling in the U.S.A. I might be in California and have to ask for directions. A native Californian might ask where I am from, as it would be obvious that I am not from there. It is one thing to say, "I'm not from around here," but to say that I am a stranger on Earth carries a whole new meaning to the term "foreigner."

King David is not the only one in Scripture who uses such expressions. Consider Abraham, who was looking for a heavenly city (Heb 11:10), or the Apostle Paul, who said our citizenship is in heaven (Phil 3:20). Peter tells us that as foreigners and strangers, we are to abstain from sinful desires in this world (1 Pet 2:11).

I don't think we can take these expressions lightly. If I truly am from another place—if my home truly is in heaven—then it only seems reasonable that my life should reflect my true citizenship. We should speak with an accent—that is, a heavenly accent. Scripture tells us that our speech should be seasoned with salt (Col 4:6) and that no corrupt communication should come from our mouths but only that which gives grace to the hearers (Eph 4:29). I really think those outside of Christ should look at us as strange, but not weird.

They should be curious about our lives, and our behavior should invite unbelievers to explore more about our true home. At least in this case, we want them to know it's okay to talk to a stranger when they are asking for directions to our homeland.

A MIND TO UNDERSTAND

I love the Psalmist's prayer, "Open my eyes that I may see wonderful things in your law" (Ps 119:18). There must be wondrous things that are buried within the text. Not all of what is written in Scripture is on the surface.

We're encouraged to seek wisdom like it's a hidden treasure. Diamonds aren't just lying around; they take real effort to uncover, which is why they're far more valuable than dirt. Here is the truly great thing about the Psalmist's prayer. The Psalmist believes that God is going to reveal some great truth that cannot be found outside of God's power to illuminate our minds to understand the deep things of Him. We are told in the Bible that, as believers, we have the Holy Spirit indwelling us. This is for the purpose of illuminating our minds so that we can understand what otherwise could not be understood. It is almost like someone inviting you into their life and sharing a secret. You feel special and trusted. You also know that what you are being told is of great value because it could never have been known had this person not shared their thoughts with you.

This is exactly what Paul tells us in 1 Corinthians 2:9-10. He says that our eyes have not seen nor have our ears heard what God has prepared for those who love Him. Now, here is the good part. He goes on to say, "But God has revealed it to us by His Spirit." It is no small matter to be invited into the personal chambers of the sovereign God of the universe and have Him confide in us some of His deepest thoughts about life and eternal matters. So, open up your Bible and ask Him to open your eyes to the truth you have never seen before. Eternal wonders await.

WHERE'S YOUR LADDER LEANING?

We have all heard the expression "rearranging the deck chairs on the Titanic." It is a very graphic picture of a business or marriage that is in such a hopeless state that all attempts to salvage it are in vain. The ship is going down. However, there is another expression that says much the same: "Their ladder is leaning up against the wrong wall." Truth be told, most of humanity has its ladder leaning up against the wrong wall. It is the wall of humanism, which basically says that if we keep leveraging our wisdom, we can correct our flaws. But what man calls "flaws," God often calls sin. Jesus made it quite clear that it is not what goes into a person that defiles them but what comes out of them (Matt 15:11). He then goes on to list a host of sins that reside in the human heart (Matt 15:10-20). Humanism wants to paint over the heart by applying the paint of education, or the paint of politics, or the paint of technology, or the paint of entertainment. But no matter how hard we try, sin continues to seep through, requiring us to apply a fresh coat over and over again.

There is another wall, however. This wall does not need to be painted. It's the wall of the gospel. Since the believer is not perfect, can sin still bleed through? No, because the sin has been forgiven, and the believer is not trusting in his or her own ability to paint over failure and sin. The person's trust is in Christ, and he or she rests in the truth that there is no condemnation to those who are in Christ Jesus (Rom 8:1).

So, make sure your ladder is leaning up against the right wall—the wall of the gospel. You simply move your ladder from trusting in your ability to turn over a new leaf or paint over the old wall and lean it up against the Cross, where total forgiveness is found. Save the paint for your front door.

TRUST

"Trust in the LORD with all your heart and lean not on your own understanding" (Prov 3:5). We love this proverb, don't we? But why is it that I am not to depend on my own understanding? We trust daily in our ability to drive a car or run a business. I doubt that many of us pray about whether we should buy an apple as opposed to an orange. So, are we leaning on our own understanding in such cases? Yes—and God would expect us to. He has given us a mind that is capable of making wise choices as we go about life.

There are moments when our desires become incredibly strong, even when we know they clash with God's will. During these tempting times, we often find ourselves leaning on our ability to reason and rationalize. We start giving ourselves counsel. "God won't mind because it's really not all that bad. I just don't see why God would say this is wrong. Everyone else seems to be doing it." In such circumstances, what we are actually doing is trying to outsmart God. We make a myriad of mental calculations to see if we can circumnavigate His will. We can't see the consequences lurking in the background. In other words, we believe the pleasure of sin far outweighs any consequence.

When we rely on our own understanding, we can count on the consequences to far outweigh any temporary pleasures. So, let's not be wise in our own eyes but fear the Lord and turn away from evil (Prov 3:7).

WHAT TIME DOES CHURCH START?

Have you ever noticed how often we, as Christians, use terminology not found in Scripture? Now I realize that all of what we say in the course of a day doesn't have to be found in the Bible. But there are terms that tend to lead all of us astray. Here is an example: "What time does church start?"

You would never find a first-century believer using such an expression because they never saw the church as being confined to a particular timeframe. Thus, they would never ask, "What time does church start?" or, "What time is church over?" The reason such expressions were never used is that they saw the church as 24/7. Church was an active community, not limited to a start time, an end time, and a location.

Of course, we need to use these terms to effectively communicate in today's language. But the reason we need to take stock in what we say is that when the church is "over," we tend to think that it is now time to be secular until the doors open next Sunday. We tend to compartmentalize, which pushes God out of our lives for six days.

The reality is that when we come together, we are just the church gathered. When we go our separate ways, we become the church scattered, living out what we've learned from Sunday morning. So, let's be careful not to separate the holy from the secular.

The church doesn't start and stop. Church IS the body of Christ. Sunday is just a more focused expression of what Monday through Saturday should look like. We don't just go to church. We are the church. All of life needs to include Jesus—not just Sunday morning. Church starts when we leave the building. This is when we become salt and light. So, the real question is not, "What time does church start?" but, "What time does church stop?"

The answer—NEVER!

MINING NUGGETS

Often, the Bible contains subtle statements that, if we really think them through, can lead us to reflect more deeply on our lives. Here is one of those seemingly passing statements found in Psalm 19. King David says that the Word of God is "more precious than gold, than much pure gold" (Psalm 19:10). So, if I take that to heart, my pursuit of mining nuggets from Scripture should outweigh my passion for making money.

Suppose the following scenario took place: You are meditating on a text, and God seems to be revealing a rich insight. There is a knock at the door, and a registered letter is handed to you. The letter from the attorney's office reveals some surprising news: your recently deceased uncle has left you a million dollars from his estate. Now, if I understand David's comment that we should desire God's Word more than gold, then our reaction should be, "I can't believe I was interrupted from my time in the Word for such a trivial matter." But let's get real—most of us would do backflips if we received such a letter. Yet David, in no unmistakable terms, tells us just the opposite should be true. We should be leaping for joy as God gives us another nugget from His Word, for that is greater than any inheritance. As a matter of fact, what He reveals to us just might save us from all the consequences that often befall those who experience sudden wealth.

So, let's not pass too quickly over God's revelation. There may be more than gold in them, their hills.

CHARACTER ON DISPLAY

As we read through Scripture, we can't help but notice a variety of remarkable people, both good and bad. The ones we most admire typically have the character to warrant our esteem.

Daniel is a perfect example. His enemies, jealous of his rise to power, tried to find flaws in his character but couldn't find any. Determined to see him dead, they hatched a plan to trap him. They went before the King and had the King agree that no one could pray to their god for thirty days, or they would be thrown into the den of lions. They knew that Daniel had such a great commitment to his God that even the threat of death would not deter his loyalty.

So herein lies the question for all of us: is our character so above reproach that if a person or group wanted to malign us, would there be any evidence to convict us? We find this in the life of Jesus. His accusers could find no basis for a charge against him (Jn 18:38). This is character on display. By display, I don't mean that we are showing off or drawing attention to our character (for that alone would be a display of poor character). I mean, that in the course of life, as we are confronted with compromising situations, we don't bend.

We don't bow to the pressure of peers or the threat of losing our jobs. We stay the course, which is admired by those who lack such conviction. Our character is showing whether we like it or not. It might even be an invitation to those around us to enter the Kingdom. As a teacher of mine once said, "Our lives should be so above reproach that should we be accused of wrongdoing, those who know us well wouldn't believe it."

FRIENDSHIPS

Can I ask a personal question? Since you can't respond, I'll assume that's a "yes." How many deep friendships do you have in your life? By "deep friendships," I mean those people with whom you can share your most personal struggles. Most people will have very few in a lifetime. If you answered two or three, that would be good.

Now, the follow-up question is, "What is the glue that holds these relationships together?" We might be tempted to answer by saying that our closest friends have the same interests as we do or that we really like their sense of humor. The reality is that personality, humor, talent, intelligence, or status don't really determine who you consider a close friend.

That's right. The glue that holds these friendships together is trust. These are people who you know are covering your back. You know they have your best interests at heart. If we were to look into Scripture, we would find that Paul tells us to consider others better than ourselves (Phil 2:3). This means that we want others to succeed in life more than we desire our own success. That has a magnetic appeal. Who doesn't want to be around people who have your success first and foremost in their mind? Most of your life is spent in trench warfare, and these are the people who live with you in the trenches. Trenches are the places where deep friendships are forged. Trenches show us a person's integrity. Simply put, integrity is character on display. Integrity is what makes you whole—a person who can be trusted. Life feels incomplete without deep friendships, and you can always rely on someone with integrity. Are you that person in someone's life?

STREET THEOLOGY

People rarely, if ever, win an argument by arguing. Jesus never seemed to get dragged into debates, though the attempts from those who opposed Him were many. They wanted to argue over taxes, divorce, inheritances, marriage in heaven, and a host of other issues. But He didn't fall for it because arguments rarely win arguments.

Jesus used what I like to call "street theology." Street theology is wisdom at its best. It goes after the real issue, not simply what is on the surface. Arguments are based mainly on saving face by stating facts. Your opponent whittles away at your logic and may have you in an intellectual headlock while all onlookers cry, "down for the count!" You know you are beat, but pride tells you that admitting defeat is out of the question. So, remember this as the headlock tightens—Jesus didn't win arguments. He won hearts. He looked for the motive. The Pharisees looked for ways to trap Jesus, and He rarely answered their questions.

The Apostle Paul tells us that people suppress the truth because of their wickedness (Rom 1:18). In other words, there are underlying issues that make us want to debate our point and win at any cost. It could be a tiff at home with a spouse or a major moral or political issue. We may be certain that those who differ with us are wrong—and they may very well be—but arguing by tossing out endless statistics and scriptural grenades will get us nowhere at blinding speed.

First, check your own heart and deal with the pride that wants to bring down your opponent. Then, listen to what the real issue is on the other side. They just might be pushing away the truth because of hidden sin. Kindness, love, and a listening ear might not win an argument, but they just might win a heart.

SO, WHO'S RIGHT?

Over the years, I've noticed that as believers grow older, they tend to follow one of two possible paths in their faith. Some people become more dogmatic in their beliefs, while others become much less so. The first group can be seen as uncompromising, while the second group might be considered liberal or lenient.

So, who is right? Our personality and church experiences largely shape the group we belong to. If you have a black-and-white view of things and notice others drifting toward liberalism, you might find yourself digging in your heels and viewing anyone who disagrees with you as a compromiser.

Your new motto is: "A compromise in secondary issues will only lead to a compromise in primary issues."

By contrast, you might be less dogmatic by nature and have seen lots of fighting over secondary issues and are willing to let some of that go in order to maintain peace.

Your motto becomes: "Live and let live."

So, who's right? Ultimately, all issues that don't directly relate to the gospel are secondary. In other words, someone's eternity isn't in jeopardy just because they prefer hymns over contemporary worship songs. However, denying the resurrection puts one's soul in jeopardy. So, when a difficult topic comes up, both sides need to step back and take a hard look at the real issue at hand. The truth in most matters of life is often found in the middle. Good, humble, healthy dialogue helps us find the center of truth.

Being open to learning is essential. God has brought us together to help navigate these issues and keep the church on the right path. I also believe God may use differences to spread out His church. Some will gather where liturgy is prominent. Others may prefer a more casual setting. Your soul is not at stake on such matters—but your humility is.

WHEN GOOD WORKS ARE BAD

As believers in Christ, we must be careful in our personal assessment of who belongs to the Kingdom and who doesn't. Yet, we must also be careful not to assume that all people who go to church are believers. After all, we are called to preach the gospel to those we come in contact with in life (1 Thes 2:4), so we need to be discerning.

Here is a question for you. If someone told you they believe Jesus is the Son of God who died on the cross to pay for sin, would you assume they are a believer? Keep in mind that many cults believe those facts, but are far from heaven. What Paul does so well is to explain that our faith must be in Christ alone. The word *alone* is key. You can believe all the facts about Christ and His resurrection, yet still trust in your good works or church membership as the reason God should let you into His family.

Paul tells us, "If by grace, then it is no longer by works; if it were, grace would no longer be grace" (Rom 11:6). He also tells us to "be found in him, not having a righteousness of my own that comes from the law, but that which is through faith in Christ—the righteousness that comes from God on the basis of faith" (Phil 3:9). Paul says that everything he used to trust in before coming to faith is now seen as a loss.

Picture a balance sheet with assets on one side and liabilities on the other. Actions like giving to the poor, attending church, and living a good life fall into the asset column. However, the moment you start relying on these assets to earn God's favor, they shift to the liability side. I call this "when good works are bad." So, what does your balance sheet look like? If Jesus is not the only listing in your assets column, now is the time to ask yourself, "Am I a true believer?"

STAGNATION

Stagnation is not usually a positive word. When food stagnates, a distinct odor becomes quite noticeable. When water stagnates, it becomes undrinkable. Sometimes, we say that our faith seems stagnant. By this, we mean that we are not moving forward. We are not maturing.

The Apostle Paul was passionate about his growth. As he put it when he wrote in Philippians, "I want to know Christ—yes to know the power of His resurrection and participation in His sufferings, becoming like him in his death" (Phil 3:10). He was driven to have a greater understanding of his Savior. I have often asked myself the question, "Why do I not have this same passion? What is hindering me from moving forward?"

When I was in the insurance business, my boss had a sign on his desk that read, "He who ceases getting better stops being good." I think we could easily apply this to the Christian life. How easy it is to look back at our progress and put the rest on cruise control. How easy to get to that place in our retirement years and say, "I have done my part; now it's time to play golf, relax, and just kick back." That, however, is not what we have been called to.

Jesus reminds us that we can be so choked by the cares and riches of this life that we bring no fruit to perfection (Luke 8:14). We must, at times, be willing to take a hard look at where we are and in what direction we are going. What are those things that have hindered us? Hebrews tells us to lay aside every weight and the sin which easily hinders us (Heb 12:1). A hindering weight may even be a good thing, but not the best thing. When carrying luggage through the airport, we find ourselves saying, "Boy, these bags are getting heavy!" The truth is, they weigh the same amount at the airport as they did at home. We are simply getting tired. So, what might you have to lay aside in order to get back in the race? The weight you are carrying may not feel heavy at the moment, but with time, exhaustion will set in—and when it does, stagnation will soon follow.

CHOICES

Here is an interesting thought: The advancement of human knowledge will always be trumped by our abuse of it. We desire to make life better by increasing our knowledge, but often the same undesirable scenario plays out in one form or another: We invent high-definition televisions that tempt us to watch more shows. Watching more shows means more snacks to enhance our viewing pleasure and less exercise. Consuming more snacks and exercising less can lead to poor health.

We are offered endless choices for every product, which often leads to conflict. If you don't believe me, just ask yourself this question: "Have I ever been in a fight with my spouse over what color to paint the living room or where to go on vacation?"

Just ask your children where they want to go for lunch, and you will get a chorus of responses from McDonald's to Burger King to Wendy's. Before you know it, a fight breaks out over what is supposed to be a good thing.

An increase in wealth has brought with it an increase in choice. And choice, which we thought was a good thing, has become the enemy. Choices keep us awake at night. What color should we paint the bedroom? What car should we buy? Should we go on a cruise or to a resort? If you've ever visited an impoverished community, you've discovered they don't fret about paint colors or where to go on vacation. The choices that keep us up at night are not available to most of the world.

For the wealthy, angst often comes with the proliferation of choices that demand decisions. We can multiply this truth out in every area of life. The advancement of human knowledge and prosperity will always be trumped by our abuse of it. The internet is a prime example. The intent may have been good, but perhaps few anticipated the resulting problems, i.e., sex trafficking, financial hacking, lack of privacy, or seeing the party you were not invited to.

Knowledge, when independent of glorifying God, will eventually glorify human beings. When we seek to glorify ourselves, God eventually gives us what we demand: to go our own way, a path that never leads to life.

LET THE PAST BE THE PAST

The Apostle Paul said, "Forgetting what is behind and straining toward what is ahead, I press on toward the goal to win the prize for which God has called me heavenward in Christ Jesus" (Phil 3:13-14). Here is what is so amazing about this: Consider what Paul had to forget. He had persecuted the church. He had people killed. How does one simply forget such things? Or do they?

The idea of forgetting does not mean that amnesia had taken over, and Paul could not remember what he had done. Similarly, when God tells us He will not remember our sins and iniquities, it does not mean He literally can't remember. It simply means the past does not control the future of our lives.

Stop living in the past. Stop allowing past failures and sin to gain control of your future. I think what Paul is really getting at is that the more passionate we are in wanting to know God, the less we dwell on the past. So, if we plan on living out the rest of our days victoriously, we must put the past behind us. Now is the time to take inventory of the past that seems to control so much of our present.

What is getting in the way of moving forward? Do we continue to revisit the same old issues that hinder our spiritual progress? If Paul could keep his past murders at bay, certainly we should be able to keep our past sins and failures in the grave. This will require some discipline.

It will mean taking a hard look at what is hindering us in our growth as a believer. It isn't just our obvious sin, but also our self-confidence and self-righteousness that need to be put in mothballs. David committed adultery, Moses murdered an Egyptian, Abraham lied, Jacob deceived, and the list goes on of people God used who had to let the past be just that—the past.

A MOST NEGLECTED TRUTH

There is a major theme that runs throughout Scripture that we often neglect. It is called The Blessed Hope. The Apostle Paul said about heaven, "And we eagerly await a Savior from there, the Lord Jesus Christ" (Phil 3:20). I have had to ask myself, "Do I live with that sort of eager expectation?" The answer is no. Each day, I wake up thinking about everything I have to deal with. However, if we examine Scripture closely, we see that most of what we experience in life should be viewed with eternity in mind. This eternal perspective is a key theme throughout Scripture.

When Paul faced trials, he said they were light and momentary when compared to eternal glory (2 Cor 4:17). When Peter wrote about temptation, he said, "Dear friends, I urge you, as foreigners and exiles, to abstain from sinful desires, which war against your soul" (1 Pet 2:11). Note how the term "foreigners" implies we are from another place. When the Apostle John spoke of materialism, he told us not to love the world or the things that are in the world (1 John 2:15). Why? Because they are passing away, but we will abide forever.

Maintaining this focus helps us stay grounded in our daily lives, as life here is so fleeting. The Scripture reminds us that life is brief, like a hand's width, a passing shadow, or grass that grows quickly but soon fades.

Or perhaps the best-known illustration is used by James when he says that life is but a vapor (Jam 4:14). Though Methuselah lived 969 years, his life was still a vapor. Let us start living in light of that which is eternal, not that which is temporal. If life is a vapor, then so are life's trials.

WHATEVER YOU DO

WHATEVER YOU DO, don't use a plastic pulpit; it's disrespectful to the word being preached.

WHATEVER YOU DO, don't use a wooden pulpit, as it makes preaching too formal.

WHATEVER YOU DO, don't do topical preaching, as it avoids the hard texts.

WHATEVER YOU DO, don't do expository preaching, as it avoids present realities.

WHATEVER YOU DO, don't wear casual attire in the pulpit. It communicates that worship is not to be taken seriously.

WHATEVER YOU DO, don't wear formal attire in the pulpit, as it highlights the haves from the have-nots.

WHATEVER YOU DO, don't use humor from the pulpit, as this draws attention to yourself.

WHATEVER YOU DO, don't avoid humor from the pulpit, as God has given us personalities to glorify Him.

WHATEVER YOU DO, don't tell stories or use illustrations from the pulpit. The Word is sufficient.

WHATEVER YOU DO, don't avoid stories or illustrations from the pulpit. Jesus told stories and illustrations are God's gracious gift for communicating, and also make the truth stick.

WHATEVER YOU DO, don't allow women to pass out communion, as this is a priestly role.

WHATEVER YOU DO, don't prevent women from passing out communion, as this allows them to be a part of the body.

WHATEVER YOU DO, don't push politics from the pulpit, as Jesus and Paul avoided this in their preaching.

WHATEVER YOU DO, don't avoid teaching politics from the pulpit as Jesus and Paul rebuked world leaders.

WHATEVER YOU DO, don't own nice things, as this is a sign of worldliness.

WHATEVER YOU DO, don't avoid nice things because God tells us He has given us all things freely to enjoy.

WHATEVER YOU DO, don't eat what is forbidden in the Old Testament, as this is God's Word for all time.

WHATEVER YOU DO, don't forbid any foods, as we are no longer under the law but under grace.

WHATEVER YOU DO, don't try and be culturally relevant, as this is a compromise and dilutes the power of God's Word.

WHATEVER YOU DO, don't avoid cultural relevance because Paul said he wanted to be all things to all men.

WHATEVER YOU DO, don't play hymns as they are outdated and do not speak to believers in this present age.

WHATEVER YOU DO, don't avoid hymns, as they have stood the test of time.

WHATEVER YOU DO, don't send your children to public school, as they will sit under the counsel of the ungodly.

WHATEVER YOU DO, don't homeschool your children because those in public school need to hear the gospel.

WHATEVER YOU DO, DON'T BE DOGMATIC WHERE there ain't no dog.

THE WORLD OF THE UNKNOWN

Have you opened the Word of God today? If so, you entered the world of the unknown. That's right. I use the term "unknown" because that is exactly why God has given us His book. It opens up a world we wouldn't know about otherwise.

Telescopic technology reveals galaxies, but it doesn't tell us where those galaxies came from or their purpose. The Word, however, says, "The heavens declare the glory of God; the skies proclaim the work of his hands" (Ps 19:1). Likewise, microscopic technology can take us into a world we cannot see with the naked eye.

The microscope, for example, shows us incredible complexity within a single human cell that's hard to imagine. Whether you're looking far out into space with a telescope or deep into tiny details with a microscope, it feels like there's no end to what you can discover. God uses the natural world to tease human minds and draw us to Himself.

Pride, however, has a way of resisting the obvious. God is screaming from the highest heavens and crying out from the depths of the sub-atomic particles within our very cells. As theologian Abraham Kuyper declared in his 1880 inaugural address, "There is not a square inch in the whole domain of our human existence over which Christ, who is Sovereign over all, does not cry, Mine!" Why do humans resist such a clear testimony of God's power and existence? Why do we resist with such ferocity? Could it be that we don't like the idea that there just might be someone out there to whom we must be accountable?

Does our pride hate the idea that someone else might be in charge? Or have we bought into the lie that "I am the master of my fate and the captain of my soul"? God is the master of all. It doesn't take much peering into the world of the unknown for that to become clear.

NATURAL vs. SPIRITUAL

"He just naturally runs fast."

"She is a natural when it comes to gymnastics."

I find it interesting that we use the word natural or naturally to define where and how people excel. I guess it's just the natural thing to do. Why don't we ever say that praying just comes spiritually to her or that Bible study just comes spiritually to him?

Since both words describe different realms, we should use them in their proper context. I believe that prayer is a function of our spirit and is therefore spiritual. Meditation is a spiritual discipline. I know it would sound funny if we started using that kind of terminology, as in, "Worshiping the Lord just comes to him spiritually." But why not? The Scripture clearly delineates the natural from the spiritual. Consider the Apostle Paul's use of these terms when he speaks of the natural person and the spiritual person in 1 Corinthians 2:6-16. The natural person is the person without Christ. The spiritual person is the one who is in Christ. Those of us who are in Christ should think spiritually as Christ thought. We have been given the mind of Christ (v. 16). This does not mean that we know all He knows, but rather that we have been given the capacity to think the way He thinks. "In your relationships with one another, have the same mindset as Christ Jesus" (Philippians 2:5).

Now, I am not really advocating that we change the way we talk, but I do think there is a subtle mixing of the two words when we say things like, "She is just a natural prayer warrior." Natural deals with our fallen state, while spiritual deals with our new birth. But then again, as the saying goes, "Old habits die hard." I suppose that too comes naturally.

LEARNING FROM OTHERS

Have you ever found yourself being overly critical of what another believer says or writes? Or maybe you've listened to a sermon and halfway through, the pastor says something you don't agree with. At that point, you probably decided that if they were wrong at one point, they must be wrong altogether, so you tuned them out for the rest of the message.

Some years ago, I recommended a book to a local pastor. I knew it was a bit controversial, but I felt it raised some good points. He read only the introduction, found one part he disagreed with, and told me he couldn't trust the author because of that one issue. Thus, he concluded from the introduction that the book would be a waste of time to read. I think we need to be careful at this point. Which of us could say that all we believe or say is one hundred percent perfect? Jesus had to rebuke his own disciples for such an attitude. The Apostle Paul said that even if Christ were being preached out of envy and rivalry, he was pleased that the gospel went forth (Philippians 1:15-18).

We can learn from people we don't always agree with. Too often, we throw out everything just because we find one point we disagree with. Of course, we need to be careful not to be led astray into false beliefs, but we also need to avoid becoming narrow-minded and overly rigid in our views. God places many people around us who have keen insight where we might be blinded. As an old saint once said to me, "The Christian life is like eating fish; you enjoy the meat and pick out the bones as you go."

BUYING AN APPLE

Most pastors feel a bit anxious when a guest speaker steps up to preach. Will they say something that doesn't align with our church's beliefs? Will they share ideas that don't quite fit with our church's values? It can be a bit nerve-wracking, and we often sit there hoping they get through the sermon without any uncomfortable moments. All of this stems from which theological lens we view life. You can't write a book or blog without it being analyzed and dissected from every theological perspective.

If someone is telling a story of how they went to the store to buy an apple, here is how it might be viewed from different theological persuasions:

The Reformed View

1. Was the purchase gospel-centered or moralistic?
2. Did God get the glory for the purchase?
3. Was the purchase of a person's free will or God's sovereign choice?
4. Was the purchaser grateful that this had been sovereignly ordained from the foundations of the world?

The Charismatic View

1. Did the Holy Spirit lead the buyer to make such a purchase?
2. Did the buyer lay hands on the fruit before purchasing?
3. Did the buyer look for bruises and ask that the fruit be healed?
4. Upon leaving the store, did the buyer raise his hands and say, "Hallelujah?"

The Mystical View

1. Did the purchaser hear from an inner voice that this was of the Lord?
2. Did they read in their devotions that morning that we are the apple of His eye, which triggered the desire for an apple?

3. When choosing, did the buyer feel a strong sense of the Lord guiding them to pick a Granny Smith instead of a Red Delicious?
4. Did the buyer have a vision of an orchard before entering the store?

The Dispensational View

1. Can such a purchase be made during the age of grace?
2. Will apples be edible during the millennium?
3. Did Adam and Eve eat an apple?
4. Were apples ripe back then? Who cares. I'm going to buy some bananas instead. Chiquita or Dole? Doesn't matter—as long as they're ripe.

CORNER ON TRUTH

Isn't it funny how we seek a second opinion from a doctor if we don't agree with the first diagnosis? We're hoping for better news, thinking maybe the first doctor got it wrong. But what about theology? Most Christians rarely look to see if there is another way to interpret a text or look into another theological system. Now, I am not advocating heresy here. I don't think we need to research whether or not Jesus came out of the grave. We are not questioning theology that has stood the test of time.

What I am talking about are more secondary issues that we have set in stone and are not willing to discuss. Keep in mind that most of what you have been fed biblically has come through a very narrow pipeline that usually consists of your family, pastor, a like-minded friend, or a theological system that you believe is flawless. Rarely do you find someone from the other side of the fence who can tell you why they believe what they believe. Iron sharpening iron isn't just for character building but for theological dialogue.

Over the years, I've changed my views on several issues after being challenged to look at Scripture from different perspectives. None of these changes impacted the gospel, but they had an impact on my life. So don't be afraid to learn from the rest of the body. Let's not stiffen up when we find that someone belongs to a denomination that we assume to be associated with false doctrine. Notice I said denomination, not cult. Looking at different perspectives can be a valuable learning experience—unless, of course, you believe you have a complete grasp on all truth.

BEING LIED TO

Since Satan is the prince of the power of the air (Ephesians 2:2), and since he is referred to by Jesus as a liar and the father of it (John 8:44), then we had better expect to be lied to a lot in this life. I don't think we need to assume that everyone we talk to is trying to pull the wool over our eyes or that no one is honest. What I do mean is that a different mindset drives the whole world system. Greed and selfish ambition lead the way. They help escort us through life, and if we are not discerning and careful, we can find ourselves trapped in the clutches of the enemy.

Here's an example of how we can be tricked. A man convinced me over the phone to set up an appointment to hear his pitch about buying meat in bulk to save a lot of money. He sat down with my wife and me, and no matter how we asked how much the meat was per pound, he managed to sidestep the issue. It was a good product, no doubt. We signed on the dotted line. But underneath all the hype was a very expensive and cleverly hidden price tag. A couple of days later, I thought of the proverb that says "the simple believe anything" (Proverbs 14:15a). I was able to get my money back due to a three-day kick-out clause in the contract.

Unfortunately, not all decisions in life come with an escape plan. When something looks too good to be true and is presented in a way that seems impossible to resist, that should be our first warning sign. Whether it is a sales pitch or clever spiel, just keep in mind there may very well be another spirit behind it. Paul tells us to not act as unwise people but as wise (Ephesians 5:15). If the father of lies is leading the world system, all decisions need to run through the Father of Truth, for this is what sets us free.

PERCENTAGE BLAME

When there is a conflict between two people, the tendency on both sides is to assign the largest percentage of blame to the other person. This is never a healthy approach to solving conflict. The real motive in this is to relieve ourselves of any wrongdoing. If most of the blame falls on them, it shifts the responsibility away from us and onto the other person in the conflict. Let's take a closer look at why this isn't a wise approach.

The following scenario is fairly typical. A husband looks at the credit card bill and fires off some harsh words at his wife for overspending. She is wounded by his response, and her excessive spending wounds him. They sit down to discuss the matter, and he believes that she is ninety percent wrong, while his harsh words only represent ten percent of the conflict. That is how he sees it. She, on the other hand, sees his words as having contributed ninety percent of the problem and assigns her spending as ten percent of the blame in their conflict. It is not hard to see that this will not be easily resolved.

The heart of most conflicts is two people seeing things very differently. None of us can fully understand life from someone else's perspective. We all face conflict, and we're usually sure that we see the issues clearly. We look at our opponents as being blind to the truth. One thing is sure: No conflict will be resolved until both sides see the truth.

If you're going through a conflict right now, be honest with yourself and admit that you don't have all the facts. And you are likely to have a limited understanding of how the other person perceives the situation.

Always go into the discussion with the attitude of "I am here to learn." So, stop playing the blame game—this will deflate the tension and make the person you're in a disagreement with feel safe enough to move toward true resolution.

ANXIOUS

In Philippians, Paul says, "Do not be anxious about anything" (Philippians 4:6). What a great exhortation. But sometimes a verse can be both comforting and troubling. This is one of them. It is comforting to know that I am not to be anxious about life and all its troubles. But the big question is, "How do I do that?"

Telling me not to be anxious is a pretty tall order. However, Paul doesn't just leave us with this exhortation. He goes on to say, "but in everything by prayer and supplication with thanksgiving let your requests be made known to God. And the peace of God, which surpasses all understanding, will guard your hearts and your minds in Christ Jesus" (Philippians 4:6-7). In other words, he calls us to replace anxiousness with prayer. You might even say that our anxiety should trigger prayer.

Scriptures call us to this kind of prayer in other places. Pray continually (1 Thessalonians 5:17); Cast all your anxiety on him, because he cares for you" (1 Peter 5:7).

What else might we expect from a perfect God?

He calls us to perfection, knowing full well that we will never achieve it in this world. All of these demands are designed to stretch us. Can you imagine the Lord saying, "Try not to worry unless it has to do with your job or health. Just relax as you wait for the biopsy results. Enjoy the weekend even though your boss chewed you out on Friday and wants to see you in his office first thing Monday morning"? These are the things we worry about. Not to worry is unnatural. Thus, prayer enters into the world of the supernatural.

I know that some of you are saying, "But I rarely get the results I want from prayer." So here is a little takeaway: Our hope is in the Lord, not the outcome. Jesus already lived all the impossible commands, died to pay for our failures, and rose to give us new life. It is this demonstration of love that causes anxiety to take a backseat as we grow in the confidence that He knows what is best.

NOT AS CLOSE AS YOU THINK

When couples fall in love, they often think their marriage will be the perfect example for others. But over time, human love can cloud our view of reality. It has a way of blinding us to the truth. It is a master of painting unrealistic pictures of life.

Now, don't get me wrong: Love is the greatest, according to Scripture (1 Corinthians 13:13). But there is a mystical side to love that tends to fog the brain. As a couple walks down the aisle, they may believe there are no barriers to their future happiness. There is a reason for this —it's called inexperience.

When a young couple, with eyes full of hope, stands before their pastor, they genuinely believe that nothing can come between them. Their vows are heartfelt, and they are dedicated to each other for the long term.

The truth is, they're not as close as they believe. The challenges of finances, sex, raising children, work, and many other unexpected issues will test any marriage and push the limits of the love they think they have for each other. I often tell young couples that if they think they can change their spouse once they are married, they had best think again. The real question is not about changing your future spouse. A better question is this: Does your love for them supersede any and all annoying habits and character flaws? If you can't say "yes" to this, then don't say "I do."

SIN BIRTHS SIN

Humanity's sinfulness tends to multiply. This is evident whenever we observe how sin leads to further sin. We might be uncomfortable with this idea, but just looking around shows us it's true. Trace the history of any criminal act, and you will see that sin often starts in a minor key and ends in a major one. King David's lust with his eyes culminated in adultery and murder (2 Samuel 11).

Here's a modern example: Imagine someone's feelings are hurt by a friend. Because of that, they start pulling away from the friendship. As they do, bitterness builds up, and they begin blaming that person for other problems in their life. Soon, the heart begins to plan ways to get back at those who caused the hurt. It could be a Facebook attack or a sarcastic tweet. Now, a small war has been declared, and sides begin to form in the former circle of friends. Harsh words (which are sinful) are tossed like grenades through social media and soon take place face-to-face.

Anger (which is sin) leads to rage (also sin), and the conflict grows worse. Evil plans are made (which is sin) and sometimes even lead to murder (clearly sin). Do you see the pattern? Sin leads to more sin, which leads to even more sin.

You can look at your own life and see how your sins lead to more of the same. Jealousy leads to hatred, which in turn causes evil thoughts. Envy leads to bitterness, which causes gossip, then anger, and eventually hostility. Sin spreads quickly, like a virus. This is why the gospel must be applied. We need to look deeply into what Christ accomplished on our behalf. Sin is not a toy but a nuclear warhead. It doesn't just affect the one who sins; it has long-range consequences. Intimacy with sin impregnates future generations. Just ask Adam.

THE FAT SOUL

I love the way the King James Version of the Bible expresses Proverbs 11:25: "The liberal soul shall be made fat" (Liberal here means generous). The idea is that the generous person has a full soul. It could be said that a greedy person has a shriveled or anemic soul. This is no small matter. There is much to say about how the Bible expresses generosity.

In the Old Testament, the rewards for generosity were usually physical. If Israel gave the first fruits of their increase in riches, then they could expect their barns to overflow with more riches (Proverbs 3:9-10). However, in the New Testament, the rewards for generosity seem to be along the lines of spiritual blessing (Philippians 4:17). Either way, God obviously knows how to give good gifts to His children, be they spiritual or physical.

Here's my concern: there's a statistic that says only about thirty percent of evangelicals give to their local church. It's hard to believe, but I think it's probably true.

How many of those who profess allegiance to Christ are living a full, robust life? Probably about thirty percent. A full life is found in generous living.

You will be fulfilled. In other words, your soul will be fat.

Too many believers are stingy. Their souls feel empty, weak, and unattractive. They know something's wrong, but they don't know why.

Generosity is giving to God what He has generously given to us. If this is not what you are experiencing, then start releasing your funds and resources for the cause of the gospel, and then step on the scales that weigh the soul. For the first time, you will be thrilled to be overweight.

THE LAW OF COMPARISON

Moses first lived in a palace in Egypt and later in a tent in the desert. The author of Hebrews tells us about Moses that "He regarded disgrace for the sake of Christ as of greater value than the treasures of Egypt, because he was looking ahead to his reward" (Hebrews 11:26). For Moses, we can surmise that living in a palace was of less value to him than living in a tent because he loved God more than materialism and power.

The Apostle Paul further expounds upon this when he says he has learned to be content whether he has plenty or is in need (Philippians 4:11-12). It is contentment that equates the great palace with the humble tent. These two structures will never be the same in value or comfort. Yet the Apostle Paul says they are equal, and the equal sign he puts between the two is the word content. Paul said he has learned to be content.

Notice the word *learned.* God had put him through many difficulties in which he learned that the riches of Christ overshadow the riches of the world. There is a specific context to his famous statement in Philippians 4:13, "I can do everything through him who gives me strength." The "everything" does not include winning a sports event, or doing well on a test, or accumulating wealth. It has to do with being content in times of abundance and in times of scarcity.

This is a significant battle in Western culture because our society has conditioned us to constantly crave more. Madison Avenue reminds us daily of all that we are lacking if we don't have their newest products. We make endless comparisons with those who have more than we do, but rarely with those who have less than we do. I call this the Law of Comparison.

Consider the fact that Christ became poor that we might be rich (2 Corinthians 8:9). The eternal riches of Christ far outweigh the temporal riches of this world, which is why Paul could say, "For to me, to live is Christ and to die is gain" (Philippians 1:21). How can living in a palace ever compare to living in a tent? Ultimately, in the context of eternity, any place where God resides is the most desirable.

FAMILY DEVOTIONS

Our culture has a strong sense of entitlement. It's almost like it's in the air we breathe. There's an unspoken belief that we owe our children the American Dream. In other words, to be a good parent, we're expected to center our lives around our kids. Their every desire is our command to play Santa Claus. I think Scripture has something to say about this. Deuteronomy 6:4-9 gives us the antithesis of passing the American Dream along to our offspring—don't build your life around your children; build your life into your children.

Now comes my confession: Here I am, a pastor telling our people week after week to get into the Word, but I have four grown children, and they will tell you (shame on me) that we never had family devotions. I think I tried formal family devotions once, and it went so badly that I decided I didn't want to force them to love Scripture. Now, I am not opposed to having family time at the altar. If you are successful at this, then more power to you. But for my family, a formal devotion time just never worked.

I went back and reread Deuteronomy 6:4-9, which is often used to support family devotions. You can certainly use it for that, but I think there is a lot more in the text. You might note that it tells parents to teach their children when they rise up, sit around, walk by the way, or lie down. It seems to me we are talking about devotions that are 24/7. That is how I approached it with my children. It was like sneaking spinach into their ice cream. We would be in the supermarket, and I would tell them about the false weight mentioned in Proverbs and false advertising. We would take walks, and I would talk of God's creative power. I wanted them to actually see how truthful the Scriptures were in real life.

So, my advice is this: Have those devotions if you can pull it off, but don't forget to sneak in some spinach as you walk.

THE COMPARISON TRAP

Sometimes, when we read a commentary or hear a message from someone who knows a great deal more about the Bible than we do, we get discouraged and question our ability to interpret Scripture. When you compare your knowledge with someone else's, you can be sure you will come up short. Here is something to think about: The issue isn't how much a scholar or pastor knows about the Bible but how much he doesn't know. What we know is finite, and what we don't know is infinite. So, what we don't know is the same as what the scholar doesn't know. If we use this as the measuring stick, everyone is on equal ground.

I have met many people who have very little formal knowledge of Scripture yet are Christ-exalting, Kingdom-advancing, neighbor-loving, victorious believers. This is not a putdown of those who have great knowledge; rather, it is an attempt to free those who feel they don't measure up because of their lack of formal training. The Spirit of the Lord is quite capable of guiding all of us into the truth. So do what King David did in Psalm 119:18-19, and pray, "Open my eyes that I may see wonderful things in your law. I am a stranger on earth; do not hide your commands from me." Keep a scholar by your side with a good commentary, but pray the prayer of David and ask the Lord to reveal the treasures of His Word. He delights in doing that.

THE ECONOMY OF MORALITY

Our country is focused on the health of its economy. When it's time to vote, the economy is usually the most important issue. Voters want to know which candidate will do the best job fixing it, especially since we don't want another stock market crash like the one in 1929. We need to avoid any depressions or recessions. We need to balance the budget and strengthen the job market. Who will lead us through whatever financial crisis we happen to be facing?

All the candidates promise big things, but there's something they seem to miss. Take the typical pie chart showing our government expenses. Each slice is a budget item denoting amounts for defense, education, and health. But what we're really looking at is just the outer crust, which hides what's really inside. How much is drained from the education budget to pay for vandalism, drug and alcohol abuse, teen pregnancy, the policing of schools, truancy, and rebellion? Look into defense spending, and a large portion is earmarked to clean up the aftermath of moral corruption. The private sector often exploits the government with excessive overrides and inflated expenses. A big part of health care goes to those who have harmed their bodies through things such as overeating, fast food, alcohol, and smoking. We can't even begin to track all the moral issues that cost this country billions every year. The pie chart shows parts of the economy, but this is just the crust, and the filling is where the money goes.

THE PUZZLE

Have you ever worked on a jigsaw puzzle? The first thing you do is look at the picture on the box. It shows you what the finished puzzle will look like. This helps you know what to look for, and as you fit the pieces together, the picture starts to take shape. But imagine if you had no idea what the picture was supposed to be. You can still fit the pieces together, but you really don't know what the final picture will be until everything is in its proper place.

Now consider what Jesus said to a couple of His disciples on the road to Emmaus just after His resurrection (Luke 24:13-35). They were downcast and confused because they had failed to grasp the fact that He had actually risen, just as He said He would. Jesus rebukes them in verse 25 and says, "How foolish you are, and how slow of heart to believe all that the prophets have spoken!" Now, this seems a bit harsh, don't you think? How were they supposed to know all about the resurrection? They had a different view of the situation—They believed Jesus had come to set them free from Roman rule.

Consider the fact that the Old Testament prophets painted two different pictures of the coming Messiah. By their accounts, Jesus was both a suffering servant and a conquering King. Prophesies about a virgin who would conceive a son (Isaiah 7:14), a serpent whose head would be crushed (Genesis 3:15), and a host of other rather vague predictions did not exactly paint a clear picture. Could anyone really find fault with the men on the road to Emmaus? After all, there was no picture on the box. The Old Testament did not display the final image on its cover. I don't think Jesus was upset because they couldn't piece together all the prophecies. But once He arrived and fulfilled all that was predicted through typology, the law, and the prophets, they should have looked at Him and seen the completed picture. Thus, He was warranted in rebuking them as "foolish."

There is also much that we read in both the Old and New Testaments that tells of Jesus' second coming. However, not all of the details are clear. We find many today who try to fit all the pieces together through various eschatological views. In the end, though, I suspect we might be surprised as to how things actually fall into place. The puzzle pieces we have so carefully laid out may get rearranged, and we might find ourselves playing the part of the men on the road to Emmaus. Prophesy is not for entertainment, but it is for those living during its fulfillment. So, let's be careful with our clever predictions. After all, who wants to be called foolish by Jesus?

QUESTIONS VS. HEARTS

Throughout Jesus' earthly ministry, a number of people tried to trap Him—not the least of whom were the Pharisees and religious leaders of His day. They often started their conversations with a question.

"Good Teacher," a rich young ruler asked "what must I do to inherit eternal life?" (Mark 10:17). Jesus replied in like manner with His own question, "Why do you call me good?" (v. 18). Then, there was the lawyer who asked Jesus what he needed to do to inherit eternal life (Luke 10:25). Here, too, Jesus answered with a question: "What is written in the Law?" (v. 26). There are a number of examples where Jesus sparred with these insincere religious leaders, but He never seemed to answer their questions. Instead, He usually asked His own questions that kept them off-balance and confused.

By contrast, when Jesus talked to the woman at the well (John 4), He offered her living water and told her to go get her husband. She responded by saying, "I have no husband" (v. 17). Jesus was quick to say, "What you have just said is quite true" (v. 18). There is a refreshing honesty here not seen in His conversations with the religious leaders. She acknowledged that He must be a prophet and perhaps the Messiah.

Why give this woman a straightforward answer but leave the religious elite scratching their heads? Their hearts were not right, and thus, any logical answer from Jesus would have been met with their intellectual counterarguments. Could there be a message here for us? I guess you could say that Jesus doesn't answer questions; He answers hearts.

WISDOM VS. KNOWLEDGE

We often mix up wisdom with smarts, thinking that a high IQ equals wisdom. But just look around—how many intelligent people make foolish choices? Intelligence is about how quickly you process information, but wisdom is knowing how to apply it.

Wisdom has several definitions. It is seeing life from God's perspective. It can be defined as the skill of living or the ability to utilize intelligence effectively. A non-Christian can be wise from the experiences of life, but never wise unto salvation (2 Timothy 3:15).

Intellect sees life as it looks on the surface. Wisdom sees life as it truly is. Our five senses help us with things like math, science, and cooking a good meal, but they don't tell us who would make the best partner, how to manage money, or what shows to watch on TV. They give us the facts, but wisdom helps us make sense of them. Wisdom guides us because it is the mind of Christ. Proverbs bids us to come and dine at wisdom's table, for there waits for us a feast. We can be a smart fool but never a wise one.

Intelligence is being close to facts, while wisdom is being close to truth. Facts aren't bad—they're helpful. We need them to make good decisions. But wisdom takes those facts and shows us the bigger picture, guiding us to the truth behind them. But facts are not enough, "There is a way that appears to be right, but in the end it leads to death" (Proverbs 14:12).

Intellect lives by the letter of the law, while wisdom lives by the spirit of the law. "Wisdom is supreme; therefore, get wisdom. Though it cost all you have, get understanding" (Proverbs 4:7).

TIME TRAVEL

Time means different things to different people. For those who love being on time, it's a strict and exact thing. But for those who are always late, time feels more like something flexible and undefined.

Therefore, terminology regarding the subject of time is interpreted very differently by both camps. Here is a comparison of the two.

"I'll be right there" to a punctual person means that within thirty seconds, they will appear. To a non-punctual person, it means that I am thinking of heading over.

"On my way" to a punctual person means they are about to pull into your driveway. To a non-punctual person, it means they are on the way but first need to get gas, then drop off some books at the library right after they grab a cup of coffee at Starbucks.

"Leaving now" to a punctual person means they are in the car, the engine is on, and they are in motion, moving in the direction of your home. To a non-punctual person, it means I am looking for my car keys, and in just another twenty minutes, the roast in the oven will be done.

"Almost there" to a punctual person means I'm on your street. To a non-punctual person, it means I'm in your state.

"Be there in a minute" to a punctual person means I'm sixty seconds away. To a non-punctual person, it means I'm in your time zone, but not sure where.

"See you in a few" to a punctual person means a few minutes. To a non-punctual person, it could mean a few hours or a few days.

"I'm just around the corner" to a punctual person means they are within a block of your home. To a non-punctual person, it means they are just around the corner from the car rental company, but will be at your place as soon as the paperwork is completed.

"Just a second" to a punctual person means they are moving as fast as they can to get out the door and be on time. To a non-punctual person, it means I still need to take a shower and figure out what I'm going to wear.

"I'll be back in a minute" to a punctual person means I am going out to the garage to get a step ladder. To a non-punctual person, it means I am going across town to rent a U-Haul.

We must learn to extend grace as we learn the language of time as expressed by others. In Scripture, an hour does not always mean sixty minutes, nor does a day always mean twenty-four hours. "But do not forget this one thing, dear friends: With the Lord, a day is like a thousand years, and a thousand years are like a day" (2 Peter 3:8).

The point of this comparison is not to berate those who are always late but to encourage both types of people to respect the others' view of time. With my military background and a metabolism that's more like a chipmunk on caffeine, I'm never late. But I've learned to be understanding toward those who have a more relaxed view of time. Let's show some grace— even if you're running out of time.

PERSPECTIVE

I've noticed that so much of how we see life comes down to perspective. Basically, the way you look at something changes how you understand it. This is true in pretty much every part of life.

Suppose you are closing on a house, and after signing all the papers, you discover a $50 error. It turns out the check written out to you for the sale of your home is $50 less than what was on the contract. You laugh and say, "I'm not going to quibble over $50 on a $450,000 sale." A few days later, you walk in from grocery shopping and find you were charged $50 too much. Will you laugh and say, "I'm not going to quibble about $50 on a $100 grocery bill?" No, you will hightail it back to the store, point out the error, and ask for a refund. Yet $50 in both cases is still $50. Perspective plays a major role in how we look at money.

Here is another example. You get a letter from the IRS saying you overpaid $500 in taxes, and you are looking at the refund check with great delight. All of a sudden, you see water dripping through your ceiling. The plumber comes out, and the bill is $500. You are crushed. "There goes the refund right down the drain." Now, let's reverse the order of events and see how perspective influences our thinking.

You spot a drip, and the plumber gives you a bill for $500. The mail arrives ten minutes later with a $500 IRS refund check. You are elated. Crushed or elated is all a matter of perspective. Try to see each event in life within its immediate context — doing so can reveal value in situations where none seemed to exist before.

BROKEN

When sin entered the world, humankind, created in God's image, became broken. Our minds became confused, our bodies weakened, and even our sense of sexuality was shattered. Though men and women still possess the image of God and are a reflection of that image, it is not at all like it was before the Fall. In the garden, Adam and Eve mirrored God's beauty and authority. After taking their cue from Satan, that reflection was shattered. This has been the cause of all the problems the world has experienced at the hands of broken people.

This profound revelation allows us to see one another as we really are. We are naked and ashamed. There really is nothing to hide. The Scriptures are quite clear that all of humanity is a mess. Jesus put it this way: "What goes into a person's mouth does not defile them, but what comes out of their mouth, that is what defiles them" (Matthew 15:11). Jesus is saying that we already have a mess inside that defiles us, or makes us unclean. He then goes on to give a long list of sins (v. 19). But our tendency is to think of those sins as done by only the most wicked people.

We think of Nero or Hitler, but that is not who Jesus had in mind. This evil heart is in Billy Graham, Mother Teresa, the Pope, and you and me. If we can grasp this, we will have a far greater capacity to extend grace to others. Until we recognize our own brokenness, we'll struggle to understand or connect with others who are also broken. Whether it's sexual struggles, emotional pain, or any other way our sinful nature shows up, we all have our broken parts.

Today, big topics like homosexuality and gay marriage are often discussed. But here's the truth: a man lusting after a woman isn't any less of a sin than a man lusting after another man. Yet, somehow, we tend to think our own brokenness is less serious than the person we're judging. We will never be able to relate to or dialogue with those who sin differently than we do if we hate them, see our sinfulness as less than theirs, or ourselves as inherently better. Homosexual sin and heterosexual sin are serious matters in the eyes of God; neither should label the other as the greater evil.

Angry insults fly through the air like arrows, which only intensifies the issue. Let's keep this in mind—*love is not to be construed as agreement, and disagreement is not to be construed as hate.* Once both sides of the issue can accept this, then and only then will we be able to move forward.

GRACE RECEIVED, GRACE APPLIED

Grace is far more than just unmerited favor. It is the power to live the Christian life (1 Corinthians 15:10). It is our instruction on how to live a God-honoring life (Titus 2:1-13). We must not see it as something we received at conversion and then put on the shelf, only to be referred to when we are giving our testimony. No! It is our very life. Paul realized he had received grace for his justification but also needed it for his sanctification. He was able to say, "Are you so foolish? After beginning by means of the Spirit, are you now trying to finish by human flesh?" (Galatians 3:3). Paul looked at life through the lens of grace.

When it came to trials and difficulties, he applied grace to his wounds. The Lord told him, "My grace is sufficient for you" (2 Corinthians 12:9).

Paul went on to say that he would glory in his infirmities so that the power of Christ may rest upon him (v. 9). This gave him a whole new perspective on how to face life. He saw his trials, which were many, as light and momentary. Paul knew he had received this grace from heaven, so he applied it in every area of his life. He then extended it to those who had yet received it. He planted churches and preached the good news of the gospel of the grace of God. That grace has now reached the whole world, and you and I are blessed enough to receive it through the words of others, whether spoken or written. We learn to apply it by drinking deeply from its cup. As it begins to overflow, we extend it to others not just by sharing the gospel but by blessing those around us through ministry.

When you look at your own life, ask yourself: Did I receive this gift of grace and then tuck it away as though it were only effective in saving my soul? Did it stop there? It must flow like a river into our lives as we face a difficult boss, a prodigal child, or a prolonged illness. It must then be shared with the rest of the world, for without the grace of God, there is no hope.

Since we are members of His kingdom, every ability, gift, and talent can be multiplied by the power of God's grace.

That grace is always available if we humble ourselves before the Lord. That is why Scripture says, "God opposes the proud but shows favor to the humble" (James 4:6).

DOUBT

Many people doubt the God of Scripture. It goes something like this: I was raised to believe that Jesus will protect me, yet I just got in a serious car accident. I was raised to believe God answers prayer, yet mine never go beyond the ceiling, and going outside doesn't work either. I have read that the Lord will do immeasurably beyond what I ask or think, but this, too, has failed. Why bother moving forward when the reality of life challenges the promises of Scripture at every turn? It all appears to be one big, gigantic hoax. I'm out of here!

There are a few fundamental problems with this kind of thinking. One has to do with the promises of God. Hebrews 11:13 says, "All these people were still living by faith when they died. They did not receive the things promised; they only saw them and welcomed them from a distance." Many of God's promises are fulfilled in the next life, not here. Secondly, we are extremely impatient and expect everything on our timetable. We are reminded to wait patiently on the Lord. That is not easy in an I-want-it-now culture. Thirdly (and I believe this is the biggest reason some leave the faith), we live in a culture that does all it can to relieve any pain, discomfort, or inconvenience. Even our medicine comes in cherry and grape flavors. So, when prayers aren't answered, or life throws us a curveball, we chuck the faith.

If you travel to countries where Christians are persecuted or have little or no food, there is virtually no questioning God's goodness. America has us bubble-wrapped, and we just don't see life as others do. The apostles went through horrific difficulties, yet there was no "Why me?" coming from their lips. When we confuse the promises of God with the false sense of security defined by the American dream, we will tend toward doubting God. But God's dream for our world is so much better than anything a nation can imagine for itself, for Jesus has overcome the world! "I have told you these things, so that in me you may have peace. In this world you will have trouble. But take heart! I have overcome the world" (John 16:33).

VITAL AND ESSENTIAL

When a doctor examines someone after an accident or when they're not breathing, the first thing they check is the vital signs—things like blood pressure, body temperature, and heart rate. Without a heartbeat, a person can't survive. It's that essential. A business cannot survive without careful financial oversight. We would say it's essential. In the Christian world, we often refer to our theological persuasion as vital or essential to a vibrant Christian life.

Yet we meet people from many different doctrinal backgrounds who are joyful, vibrant believers. Two people living God-honoring, kingdom-advancing, Christ-exalting lives who hold to different theological systems only prove that those cherished beliefs cannot be vital or essential. However, one cannot live a Christ-glorifying life and deny the resurrection or salvation by grace through faith.

When we stick too rigidly to our own narrow views of theology, claiming we're the only ones with the right answers, all we do is create more division. Without mixing ideas and learning from others, we end up stuck in a cycle of only hearing from ourselves, which always results in something flawed.

Just take a look at church history. People killed each other over differing views on baptism. This is why theological movements attract the same kind of people. The movement eventually dies out because doctrine becomes so thinly sliced that the potential for disagreement increases exponentially, and proponents of the movement splinter into oblivion.

Keep the resurrected Christ at the center, along with those doctrines that are vital and essential to real life, and the unanswered prayer of Jesus "that we might be one" just might get answered.

IF I ONLY KNEW

One of the favorite verses in the Bible for those who don't necessarily hold the Bible in high esteem is Matthew 7:1-2, "Do not judge..." Now, if you are not familiar with this verse, it might be because it is, in fact, not a verse but only part of one. The actual statement from Jesus is, "Do not judge, or you too will be judged."

The basic context is to tell us that we should not judge others while ignoring our own faults. Jesus isn't saying this because we don't know the whole story about others, but because we each have issues in our own lives that must be dealt with first. "You hypocrite, first take the plank out of your own eye, and then you will see clearly to remove the speck from your brother's eye" (Matthew 7:5). So, let's consider what Jesus is teaching us. We would be far less judgmental if we only knew. If we only knew the story behind the one we are judging. Perhaps they come from a broken family. Perhaps they were sexually abused as a child, or were exposed to an angry alcoholic father, or were belittled by a coach or teacher. All of life's experiences shape who we are. Many people deal with bitterness, anger, fear, social anxiety, hatred, and a host of other spiritual maladies. Telling them to get over it by quoting a Bible verse does very little to relieve the struggle. Yes, we are all morally responsible for our actions, but many of our actions and sinful behavior have been modeled for us. Perhaps if we saw people as Jesus did, we would have a different perspective. He was never irritated or frustrated by people's behavior. Only the self-righteous behavior of the Pharisees set Him off. Prostitutes, gluttons, tax collectors, and sinners of every stripe were drawn to Him.

When we are being judged, we want to say to those judging, "If you only knew." If we only knew the other person's story, we might be less angry and more compassionate. And wouldn't that make the church very attractive?

LOOKING FOR A CITY

What is the church to do in the midst of moral decay? Are we called to tell the world how to live? Is the church to act as a moral barometer? I think the Christian community is a bit divided on this issue. There are a few words Scripture uses that have helped me approach this issue. As believers, we are called strangers, sojourners, pilgrims, and ambassadors. The strong implication is that we have another citizenship, and like Abraham, we are looking for a city "with foundations, whose architect and builder is God" (Hebrews 11:10). So, I think the question is this: As visitors on this planet, do we have the right to tell those who are citizens of this world how to live? "What business is it of mine to judge those outside the church? Are you not to judge those inside? God will judge those outside" (1Cor. 5:12). Does a Frenchman visiting Italy have the right to tell Italians how to live? Clearly not.

The church is not called to be a moral police force but a moral example. Moral depravity bears observable consequences in the lives of those who engage in this philosophy of life. It is equally true that a godly life bears observable fruit. When the church at large is seen and not heard, it earns the right to be heard. A righteous life becomes a platform on which to preach the gospel. A compelling life of love is the ultimate apologetic. Marching with signs that condemn the world is the ultimate turnoff.

Pick someone from outside the Kingdom to invest in, and don't judge or criticize their way of life. Let them judge yours and see how much better life is in the Kingdom. Who knows, they might start searching for the same city Abraham was looking for.

CONSCIENCE

Scripture just might challenge the wisdom of Jiminy Cricket when he said, "Let your conscience be your guide." The word conscience means "to know with," and a conscience is a very trustworthy guide when programmed correctly. Perhaps this is why Paul talked about the renewing of our mind (Romans 12:2). The conscience can be wrongly programmed. If your religious authority has told you that eating cream on Saturday afternoon is a sin, then your conscience will register guilt if you violate this legalistic standard. The conscience serves as a reliable guide, shaped by the way it has been programmed. Thus, we need to have it biblically aligned. God desires us to live a life free of outside influences that are far removed from biblical truth. The world, along with its beliefs and religions, affects our conscience more than we realize. Not living up to strict rules set by religious leaders can lead to unnecessary guilt and spiritual depression.

Here are a few diagnostic questions to check the reliability of your conscience. Do you feel the Christian life is a stranglehold where you can't do this and you can't do that? Do you feel God doesn't love you if you sin? Do you feel that you need to earn God's love? If you answered yes, then chances are your conscience has been wrongly programmed.

Time to renew the mind and recalibrate your conscience to True North. Meditate on this: While religion tells you to keep God's law and He will accept you, the gospel says Christ kept the law perfectly for us so we can be accepted. Now, that's food for thought that feeds a good conscience.

BUT WHAT SAITH THE SCRIPTURES?

In the midst of Christian debates about various doctrinal issues, I have often heard this question bantered about: "But what saith the Scriptures?" This archaic expression, formed as a question, is used to imply that the Word backs our view and not our opponent's. The problem comes to a head when both sides throw this out to better leverage their position. But in reality, what we mean is: "But what saith the Scripture as I understand the Scripture?"

Now, let me be perfectly clear—I believe the Bible to be the inerrant Word of God, but I do not believe that a person is inerrant in his or her interpretation of the Word. So here is what it sounds like: "They believe in baptism by immersion, but what saith the Scripture?" Or, "They believe in a literal millennium, but what saith the Scripture?" Such statements have been cast about for as long as the church has been around. I think we need to take stock of how this question is posed. If someone denies the resurrection, then "But what saith the Scriptures?" is very valid. If someone denies that speaking in tongues still exists, then it is time for both sides to sit down and have a healthy dialogue.

Obviously, we may not all agree on what is a major issue and what is a minor one, but any doctrine that directly relates to the gospel needs to be met with careful scrutiny. For other issues, let's be open-minded in the midst of discussing our varied interpretations of the Bible. We just might find that Scripture "saith" something we never knew. Wouldn't that be refreshing?

EXCLUSIVITY

As I read the Bible, I'm always amazed at how the Lord gently shows us His heart. When I first became a Christian, I had many doubts about whether I had the truth since other religions also claimed to have the truth. What confused me the most was when I heard about someone in a cult who received an incredible answer to their prayer. The fiery darts of doubt from the enemy would break into my mind and say, "See, others claim they have the truth, and equally amazing things happen to them. Are you sure Christianity is the truth? These other groups also use the Bible, so who are you to claim you have the truth?"

Through many years of study, meditation, and teaching, I have total confidence in God's Word and the truth of His gospel. But what about these issues that have been raised? In Deuteronomy 12:20-13:4, the Lord warns Israel not to even inquire about other gods, even if their followers have amazing things happen. He tells us that signs and wonders may occur in order to test us in our love for the one true God. Asking too many questions can put us at risk of losing our faith and falling into false doctrine. I realized years ago that many have come to know Christ as Savior simply by reading the Bible. They were never told what to believe, nor were they indoctrinated into a system of belief, but the Holy Spirit led them to discover the basic truths of the faith. This cannot be said of cults or false religions. For example, no one would arrive at the doctrines of Mormonism by reading the Bible alone; those teachings come from the Book of Mormon. They must be carefully led into a certain way of thinking. There is a literal brainwashing that takes place because there is no Spirit of God to reveal the truth of Scripture.

I hope this helps anyone who has struggled with such doubts. Stay in the Bible and let the Holy Spirit guide you to the truth.

MISSIONS

Missions are the heart of God. It's...

Souls, not self

Others, not me

Substance, not surface

Eternal, not temporal

Releasing, not restraining

Vision, not viewing

Sacrifice, not comfort

Missions are the heart of the church. It's...

Caring and bearing

Here and there

Giving and getting

Praying and praising

Sowing and reaping

You and me

Missions are the bottom line of bottom lines. It's why we as a church exist. It's the cure, not the cause, of what ails all peoples of the world. Missions are medicine to the masses. It's the panacea for the plague. It's hope for the helpless. It's God's gift. It's an invitation to the wedding feast. Missions are God's gift—the invitation to the wedding feast. The question is, will they be there too? Selah.

APPROACHING THE WORD

1. Approach the Word with the understanding that it is spiritually, not intellectually, discerned. "The person without the Spirit does not accept the things that come from the Spirit of God but considers them foolish, and cannot understand them because they are discerned only through the Spirit" (1 Corinthians 2:14).

2. Approach the Word prayerfully. "Cause me to understand the way of your precepts; that I may meditate on your wonderful deeds" (Psalm 119:27).

3. Approach the Word with all the reverence of approaching God Himself. "Rulers persecute me without cause, but my heart trembles at your word" (Psalm 119:161).

4. Approach the Word with the expectation of hearing from God. "Open my eyes that I may see wonderful things in your law" (Psalm 119:18).

5. Approach the Word with the understanding that it is built precept upon precept: 'Do and do, do and do, rule on rule, rule on rule; a little here, a little there' (Isaiah 28:10).

6. Approach the Word by listening to what it says about itself. "Your word is a lamp to my feet, a light on my path" (Psalm 119:105).

7. Approach the Word with the resolve that you will obey what it says. "Teach me, LORD, the way of your decrees, that I may follow it to the end. Give me understanding, so that I may keep your law and obey it with all my heart" (Psalm 119:33-34).

8. Approach the Word through the doorway of affliction. "It was good for me to be afflicted so that I might learn your decrees" (Psalm 119:71).

9. Approach the Word through meditation. "But whose delight is in the law of the LORD, and who meditates on his law day and night" (Psalm 1:2).

10. Approach the Word through study. "Do your best to present yourself to God as one approved, a workman who does not need to be ashamed and who correctly handles the word of truth" (2 Timothy 2:15)

IF I WERE EMPATHETIC

Being empathetic does not mean that I am to carry the weight of the world's problems. This is not reasonable and certainly not practical for one simple reason—all the world is hurting. The context of life is a world of pain and need. This does not, however, excuse me from being empathetic. Empathy has boundaries, and two things come into play for it to be carried out—proximity and familiarity. In Paul's second letter to the Corinthians, we find in the first chapter that we are to comfort others the same way we have been comforted by the Lord (2 Corinthians 1:4).

This implies that two conditions must be met if empathy is to transpire. First, I have to be in the vicinity of the one I am to give comfort to. Second, I am best equipped to minister if I have been through a similar heartache. I can easily let myself off the hook if these two don't line up. However, if I am truly empathetic, there is another way to do this. I can find someone who does qualify and encourage them to come alongside the wounded party. "I am sending him to you for this very purpose, that you may know how we are, and that he may encourage you" (Ephesians 6:22). In such cases, I am showing the love of Christ.

I will never care for those who are hurting as much as I should. However, there is someone who did more than just stop to help. There is someone who has been touched by the feelings of our infirmities. There is someone who has suffered spiritual, emotional, and physical wounding. Where I have failed, He has triumphed, and in this triumph, I am moved to be like Him. When I am like Him, I will be empathetic. His name is Jesus.

VISION CASTING

"Vision casting" is a popular term in the world of church growth. I like the term, but I think we need to be sure what we mean. First and foremost is the fact that Scripture is strongly in opposition to vision casting when it proceeds from our own will. God is the supreme vision-caster. Let's take a look at God's vision for Abraham found in Genesis 12, where the Lord told Abraham that he would be the father of a great nation. When no child came, Abraham's wife, Sarah, decided to help God out and cast her own vision. This included giving her maidservant Hagar to her husband Abraham so Sarah could take that child as her own (Genesis 16:2). This vision was from the flesh. She had not heard from God but made her own plans, which resulted in serious consequences.

So, how do I know whether my vision is from God or just another line item in my agenda for success? Vision stems from passion. When the Lord gives you a passion to advance His kingdom, several things will be true:

1. The passion will not be for your glory but His.
2. His Spirit will drive you to carry it out.
3. It will be consistent with the big vision of Scripture and will never contradict Scripture.
4. It will require God's power.
5. You will not feel satisfied until it is fulfilled.
6. It will be about Him and not about you.

God's grace will cast God's vision and empower you to fulfill it in His time, in His way, for His glory.

A DIM VIEW OF REALITY

Paul tells us that we see through a mirror dimly, but eventually we will see God face to face (1 Corinthians 13:12). What is dim or unclear? Though Paul doesn't spell it out, we know that our own life experiences don't always square with Scripture. We are puzzled by many of life's strange twists. We see and hear things that don't seem to match what God says. He promises that He will never leave us or abandon us, but many situations in life make it hard to see that promise clearly.

When the Lord clearly defined the parameters for Adam and Eve regarding the forbidden tree, what dimmed their understanding? Satan offered another interpretation of God's clear command not to eat the fruit. Through sin, darkness came over the human soul. Redemption brings back the light, but darkness still lingers inside us. Abraham understood God's call and left his homeland, but fear soon made him doubt it as he worried for his life when entering Egypt. Saul understood God's call, but disobedience and jealousy made him lose sight of God's clear instructions. Anger got the best of Moses, and watching wicked people prosper veiled the eyes of Asaph. Simply put, sin keeps us from seeing Him clearly. Paul goes on to say we see dimly now, "but then face to face." This is an expression of clarity. What will we have in Heaven that will give us such clarity? Lack of sin and the presence of Christ.

We have a principle here. The more obedient we are, the more clarity we have in this life. The fog will never completely lift until heaven, but as we follow Him closely, we will see more clearly.

TREASURING STUFF

"Honey, will you get my stuff on the bed and put it in the closet? While you're at it, could you get the stuff out of the back seat of the car and dump it in the garage?" I don't know how many times a day we use the word stuff, but I suspect it's more often than we think. It's a filler word for those things that are now getting in the way of a productive life. Stuff is what we wish we could unload, but there is just too much of it that we don't know where to begin. The word carries a wide variety of meanings, from all the "stuff" in the basement to all the "stuff" we have to do at the office. Note that this word is never used for that which we value. The Hope Diamond is never called "stuff." A new purse is not called "stuff," nor is a new set of golf clubs.

So, what turns treasures into stuff? When they lose their luster. Jesus referred to this when He said not to lay up treasures on earth where moth and rust corrupt (Matthew 5:19). Treasures become stuff when they are outdated or out of style. The new car becomes stuff when it is no longer the topic of conversation in the neighborhood. Treasures become stuff when a newer model shows up. Treasures become stuff when we realize we brought nothing into this world and we will carry nothing out (1 Timothy 6:7). Treasures become stuff when they no longer bring us the pleasure they once did. Treasures become stuff when they wind up at our spring yard sale. We put new price tags on old treasures. The treasured gas grill we paid $400 for is now going for $40 because it is no longer a prized treasure—now it's just stuff. So, just how much stuff do we have?

Ultimately, treasures become stuff when we leave this world. Jesus reminded us of that when He told the parable of the rich fool who had built bigger barns to keep all his stuff in. "This very night your life will be demanded from you. Then who will get what you have prepared for yourself?" (Luke 12:20). Remember that all your present treasures are future stuff. Steward that which is eternal.

TRAJECTORY

The Bible has a trajectory. It tells a story with a moving plot line. The story is about Jesus. The launching pad is Genesis 3:15, which predicts His birth and wounding. The landing is Matthew 28:6, declaring His resurrection. Everything in between is the trajectory that foretells His coming. The Patriarchs point to Jesus. Adam was a type of Christ in reverse. Through Adam came sin and death; through Christ came righteousness and life.

Noah is next in line as he obeys God and builds an ark. The ark would take those on board from the world that then was to the world that now is. It was the only way to be saved physically and spiritually. All of these points to Christ as the only way to heaven.

Abraham is called from his pagan background to be the father of all who believe. God's covenant with Abraham points to Christ because, through Abraham, all the nations would be blessed—and this blessing is the Messiah.

Isaac is the promised seed and is offered up as a sacrifice. He is Abraham's son, his only son. All of this foreshadows Jesus as God's only Son, who was the ultimate sacrifice.

Jacob is next up. His tragic life becomes part of the very line through which the Savior comes. Though not as much a type of Christ, Jacob represents the kind of broken people God uses in His redemptive plan.

Later, just before Joseph reveals himself to his brothers, Judah steps up and offers to take the place of his younger brother, Benjamin, as a pledge. Christ steps in to be our substitute. Judah becomes a type of savior for his people, pointing us to Christ as the Savior of the world.

On and on, the story unfolds, each chapter pointing to Christ, who is the Anointed One. The trajectory is undeniable. As you read through the Bible, ask the Holy Spirit to help you spot these glorious mile-markers.

MANGLING THE TRUTH

The most powerful verse in all of Scripture that explains why truth is reinvented, twisted, distorted, and mangled beyond recognition is Romans 1:18, which states: "The wrath of God is being revealed from heaven against all the godlessness and wickedness of people, who suppress the truth by their wickedness." Humanity takes what is obviously true and ignores it so we can do as we please. We creatively resist God's authority. Simply put, Romans 1:18 is God's way of telling us why we don't like the truth. It gets in the way of our autonomy and perceived freedom.

It explains why the Bible is now being reinterpreted on subjects that have stood the test of time but failed to stand the test of lust. For instance, several years ago, Facebook lit up with professing believers recommending *Fifty Shades of Grey*. Evangelicals caved on the issue of same-sex marriage. Holiness is now considered legalism.

Why weren't these ideals promoted decades before they became commonplace? What made politicians who affirmed traditional marriage so quickly change their minds? Why didn't these champions of truth and justice speak up in the '90s? For corporate America, it was undoubtedly *cha-ching!* Had they pushed too early on the issue while America was trying to make up its mind, they would have lost billions. Now that America has decided, corporate America has taken what it thought to be true twenty years ago and decided it is no longer true. The politicians would have lost every election if they proposed then what we accept now. They put their political finger to the wind and noticed not just a slight breeze but a gale-force wind that turned their rigid backbone into that of a jellyfish. Money and votes give birth to passion, which, in turn, flips the truth on its head.

Sadly, many modern evangelicals are so afraid of being called narrow-minded bigots that they have now abandoned their beliefs. Rest assured, however, this shift in moral values has not taken Scripture by surprise. Such abandonment of truth might surprise us, but Scripture has said it all along—the fear of man brings a snare (Proverbs 29:25).

ROBUST THEOLOGY

Many blogs, books, and articles are circulating throughout the evangelical world talking about the need for robust theology. The Reformed camp, in particular, wants to protect sound doctrine from being diluted. This is certainly a worthy cause. Statements such as, "I love Jesus; I just don't care for doctrine," meet with much dismay among those of us who love meaty theology. After all, how can you truly love Jesus if you don't know the doctrines that reveal Him? Those who claim to love Jesus but avoid theology are often faced with the question: 'Which Jesus do you love?'

Suppose the following reply comes back. "I love the sovereign God who sent His Son to pay for the wages of sin, which is death. I believe that Jesus took my place and absorbed the Father's wrath that was meant for me. I believe that His righteousness was placed to my account, and I will stand before God as forgiven because of His Son's sacrifice on my behalf."

Does that qualify as robust theology? How much more does that person need to know? So, the question that needs to be answered is: What constitutes robust theology? It reminds me of a famous quote often attributed to Augustine, "In major things unity, in minor things liberty, in all things love." We are again faced with the obvious question: What is major and what is minor? Now think about how few Christians have ever heard of limited atonement, let alone know what it means. Tell a Pentecostal that the second blessing is not important, and they'll probably want to lay hands on you in more ways than one. Again, most believers don't even know what that means.

So, we find ourselves trying to figure out just what we need to know in order to live a "robust" Christian life that, according to some, must be tethered to robust theology. Yet, we find many Christians living a robust life with different definitions of robust theology. Go figure.

Simple logic leads us to the conclusion that people can have an intimate relationship with the Lord and believe different things about Him, even contradictory things. No one could possibly be one hundred percent correct in their theology. I had the great privilege to sit under the teaching of J.I. Packer at a conference on the Holy Spirit over forty-five years ago. During a Q&A session, someone asked him how God could possibly bless a certain denomination when they are so doctrinally off. He responded by saying, "I'm off doctrinally. I just don't know where." I will never forget that humble reply, which has stuck with me over the years.

We often say there are mature believers on both sides of a doctrinal debate. If true, then the issue is likely not of great importance. I asked Dr Packer if he believed God could look down and say, "Now that's a church!"? Without hesitation, he said, "Yes, and it's probably meeting in a cave in Nepal." Those two statements have stuck with me over all these years.

THE GOSPEL

Wouldn't you think that by now we would know what the gospel is? This is another subject that splits churches and creates division. The gospel can be presented in numerous ways, with everyone thinking they have the exact irreducible minimum amount of information for a person to enter the Kingdom. Have you ever noticed in Scripture that the gospel is never given the same way twice?

In John 3, Jesus tells Nicodemus he must be born again. In John 4, Jesus tells the woman at the well is to drink the water that leads to eternal life, yet nothing is said about being born again. In John 6, Jesus tells His listeners to eat His flesh and drink His blood for eternal life, but nothing is said about being born again or drinking the water that leads to eternal life. In John 9, Jesus asks a blind man if he believes in the Son of Man, but He says nothing about what He told the other three people. In John 11, He tells Martha to believe that He is the resurrection and the life, and if she believed, she would never die. The gospel is then presented in 1 Corinthians 15 as Jesus's death and resurrection from the grave. So, which one of these is the gospel?

The gospel is hard to define because it isn't just information, it's a Person. Jesus is eternal life. Yes, we must believe in certain truths, such as the resurrection—without it, we are the most miserable of all people. Yet I hesitate to speak of an irreducible minimum, because a person cannot be reduced to mere information about Him. Remember, most cults affirm Christ's death and resurrection, yet remain far from the Kingdom of God. Why? Because their confidence rests not in Christ but in themselves. Every religion in the world points to human effort for salvation, but that very effort becomes its condemnation. The gospel, by contrast, is good news for the broken and bad news for the self-righteous. Let's keep it good.

APPLYING THE GOSPEL

The gospel not only saves us, but is the basis for daily living. When I think of what was accomplished on my behalf at Calvary, four things come to mind. The gospel is all about humility, sacrifice, love, and grace. We must get in the habit of applying these to everyday life when relating to others. No matter what the issue or who the person is, these powerful virtues will not only change us, but will also change those around us.

Marriage is a great place to practice this truth. Most arguments happen when we forget these four things. For example, the wife wants to go out to dinner after spending the whole day taking care of the kids. Meanwhile, the husband is tired from a long day at work and wants to have a quiet meal at home. If both choose to be loving, humble, sacrificial, and grace-filled, do they go out or stay home? The beauty of the gospel is that the Lord will decide. A disagreement can't happen when the Holy Spirit leads both parties (Husbands, get ready to go out).

It's often the leader's job to set the pace in these situations. An employer who leads with humility, sacrifice, love, and grace will have many happy employees. The coach who makes his players a priority in his life will have a team that desires to work together and make each other successful. Hogging the ball is no longer an option. Parents who establish loving virtues as a pattern in their lives will have children who see their benefits.

The church, in particular, needs to be an exemplary model of these characteristics. The gospel saves the church and gives it the power to be loving, humble, sacrificial, and gracious. So, take inventory and see if this is being lived out in your life. There was an ad years ago that said, "I use Dial. Don't you wish everybody did?" Great ad. Suppose we could all say, "I apply the gospel to all my relationships. Don't you wish everybody did?"

LINKED

Life is so interconnected. The tongue, for example, is linked to the heart; "For the mouth speaks what the heart is full of" (Matthew 12:34b). Our thoughts are linked to the essence of who we are: "For as he thinks in his heart, so is he" (Proverbs 23:7, NKJV).

We must always remember that our words, thoughts, and actions have a ripple effect that reaches far beyond the moment. A harsh word that hurts another person may cause the friend of the offended person to retaliate. The reverse is true as well. Humility has a positive chain reaction. A humble person is a safe person whom others find hope in. Humility is a receptacle of grace. "God opposes the proud but shows favor to the humble" (James 4:6).

See yourself as a gospel link. Fifty years ago, I was shining shoes at a local country club. One day, I heard the sound of cleats hitting the counter. I looked up and lo and behold, it was a classmate from college. Talk about being embarrassed. He invited my wife and me over for dinner. I gave him the gospel. He wasn't interested. A few years later, our paths crossed, and I shared my faith again. His interest was piqued, but nothing more appeared to come from our encounter. However, he later emailed me about a man in hospice whom he had been witnessing to, but had seen little response. My friend wanted to know if I would call this man and give him the gospel. I was blown away—my old classmate had become a believer and was sharing the gospel! I called the man in hospice, shared the gospel, and he received Christ. The connection went back fifty years. God works through these connections to bring redemption, many of which we will never fully understand until we reach heaven.

LISTENING VS. HEARING

"Did you hear me?" is an oft-repeated question in the midst of a heated conversation. What the questioner has in mind is, "Do you understand what I said?" James 1:20 says, "Human anger does not produce the righteousness that God desires." This may be the most practical advice about communication ever given. Most of us talk over one another. We begin by listening to the other side, but soon we start planning how to defend ourselves. At that moment, the listening stops.

Hearing and listening are two very different skill sets. Hearing has to do with our physical ability. We hear people speak words because our ears detect sound waves. Words have meaning and are understood not merely by one's ability to hear but also by the ability to translate what one hears. Listening, however, is the translation of those waves into understanding. I heard what you said, and I understand what you said because I value your thoughts.

If, on the other hand, we are quick to gather our arsenal of words to defend ourselves, we have officially stopped listening and have missed the point the other person is trying to make. Pride is usually at the helm, steering the ship in such cases.

This is why James says, "Everyone should be quick to listen, slow to speak and slow to become angry." How many arguments could be avoided if we followed this simple advice? How many marriages saved, and friendships restored? Just three little words—swift to listen—are sharper than any sword. In fact, if we truly lived by them, we would have no need for swords at all.

TWO WORDS THAT MAKE A DIFFERENCE

The number of students who have been raised in a good home, a good church, and a solid youth group who leave their faith when they enter college is well over fifty percent, according to recent surveys. How can this be? Many studies have been done, but there seems to be little consensus as to what the underlying cause is.

It is often said that science teachers and philosophy professors make young people doubt the accuracy of the Bible, particularly when it comes to topics like the origin of life or its meaning. So, imagine an eighteen-year-old freshman sitting before a teacher who has a doctorate in biochemistry and mocks the Scriptures. How can this even be a challenge? This is David and Goliath, and David has neither a stone nor a sling. A semester of bullying by the professor who offers proof of evolution begins to erode the faith of this young man or woman. No matter how well-equipped the student is with apologetics, the professor is several steps ahead and will soon prove to this naive teen that he has been shielded from the truth and has been brainwashed inside the evangelical bubble. It's time for him to grow up, face the real world of science, and leave behind make-believe. Now that the student's faith has been shaken, it's easier to give in to sexual temptation because he feels there's no God to answer to.

How did eighteen years of solid teaching get erased in six months? Here's how. Over the years, two words have blended and now have the same meaning. This blending has done untold damage to young and old minds alike. The two words are science and scientist. Somehow, over the years, these two words became one and the same. So, if a scientist makes a claim, it soon becomes the inerrant voice of science. Let's put some definitions to these words. A scientist is a fallible interpreter of experimentation and observation. Science is an infallible interpreter because it is backed by what is observable and reproducible. We know, for example, that water boils at 212 degrees Fahrenheit at one atmosphere of pressure at sea level, and it does it every time. However, in those areas that are subjective and cannot be put to objective experimentation, the words science and scientist are used interchangeably. For example, twenty-five years ago, it was a known fact that cholesterol was the major cause of heart disease. Today, the scientific community has corrected that error by saying that sugar is the main culprit. These types of studies are wide open to interpretation since they are not observable, measurable, or reproducible. Which science is the right one? The science of twenty-five years ago or the science of today? Since science, by definition, is provable and thus factual, I think it is safe to say that at least one (if not both) of these interpretations of the available data is wrong.

However, when a scientist says that studies prove this or that about heart disease, it becomes science; these two words are now synonyms when, in many cases, they are really antonyms. Evolution and the study of origins fall into the category of looking into the rear-view mirror and trying to interpret the past. But to a young, naive college student who hears his prof say that evolution is an undeniable fact, he takes the bait, swallows the hook, and chucks the faith—all because he failed to understand the difference between science and scientist. So, let's help our young people put on their big boy pants and learn the difference between an antonym and a synonym. It just might save their faith.

THE GENIUS OF THE ADAMIC NATURE

When my granddaughter Holland was two and a half, her mother told her not to do something. With great vocal defiance, Holland said, "No!" She was gently corrected. After the discipline and not to be outdone, she looked at her mother and said, in a muted tone, "No." The discipline was repeated, only to be followed by repeated defiance. After the final correction, Holland didn't say "No" loudly, nor did she speak it softly. She simply mouthed *Noooo*.

Now follow me as we travel into the innocent little heart of Holland. She can barely converse. She can't do math. She knows nothing about logic or methods of debate, yet she could figure out that saying "No" in loud or soft tones was a violation of her mother's law. She also figured that mouthing it technically didn't violate the letter of the law, but knew full well that it violated the spirit of the law. How could such a sweet little child with no real experience in life be so clever and manipulative? Think of all the calculations her mind had to go through to pull this off. Think of her clear understanding of right and wrong and how she might test the limits.

Holland's cousin Harper, who was three at the time, hollered at her father from her crib, "You're a bad daddy!" My son looked her in the eye and said, "What did you just say?" Her quick mind responded with, "I said I was having a bad day." Now, let's analyze this pattern of thinking. She had a split second to find two words, bad day, that rhyme with bad daddy. If the IQ to sin could be transferred to the world of science, these two little munchkins, along with all other children, would be teaching at MIT.

Where did this brilliance for defiance come from? How do they know which buttons to push and how hard? This is the genius of the Adamic nature. When Adam said "No" to his Creator, he passed it on to the human race, who have learned to say "No" to God loudly, softly, and silently. Someday, I trust Holland and Harper will say "Yes" to Jesus, and when they do, every "No" will be forgiven—and they just might change the world.

TESTIMONIES ARE NOT FORMULAS

A number of years ago, I was reading an article on faith. It was not a name-it-and-claim-it type of faith that was being presented, but it might as well have been. It was the testimony of a young couple who were not able to conceive in spite of all the medical expertise available. Needless to say, this was very discouraging, and no hope was in sight.

Someone suggested they prepare a bedroom for a baby as a demonstration of their faith in God. Within a few days, the wife became pregnant, and within nine months, they had their first child. Praise God!

The gist of the article was that when we step out in faith and believe in God, great things will happen. I couldn't help but wonder how many childless couples followed this testimony as though it were a formula. How many hopeful couples wound up with a pink or blue bedroom and crib but no one to fill it? How devastating. Testimonies are great, and I love to hear them—but they are not formulas. Otherwise, all of us would have Red Sea or burning bush experiences.

Many have been disillusioned by following someone else's testimony as though it were a formula. Many have said a certain prayer for deliverance but saw no results, even though someone else testified of how enslaved they were until they prayed a certain prayer. What has worked for you may not work for someone else, and vice versa. God is creative and almost never does things the same way twice. So trust Him to work in your life as He chooses, and don't compare it to how He works in someone else's life. Testimonies are not a set formula.

JOSEPH AND JONAH

Joseph and Jonah couldn't be more opposite. Joseph had no choice but to go along with God's plan as he was sold into slavery (Genesis 45:5). Jonah, on the other hand, was called by God to head east, but he went west.

Then there was a strange twist that, at first glance, makes no sense: They both suffer. One suffers in the midst of obedience, and the other in the midst of disobedience. Joseph flees from an immoral woman, but as a result of his godly moral compass, he winds up in prison. Not only does he not complain or shake his fist at God, but he ministers to the other two prisoners by telling them that God can reveal their dreams. Jonah didn't flee from an immoral woman but from God, and he found himself imprisoned in a great fish.

Both men suffered, but for different reasons. Joseph's suffering was clearly ordained by God and played a major role in redemptive history. Jonah's suffering was the result of God's disciplinary hand and pointed to the One who is the culmination of redemptive history (Matthew 12:40).

Jonah knew full well why he was suffering, but how could Joseph know? He had obeyed, and it stands to reason that if we obey, God will reward us. For Joseph, there seemed to be no rhyme or reason. It wasn't until later in his life that he could see some of the pieces falling into place. This is born out in his famous statement as he addressed his brothers, "You intended to harm me, but God intended it for good to accomplish what is now being done, the saving of many lives." (Genesis 50:20).

Once Jonah was delivered from the fish, he also saw God's hand when he confessed, "I knew that you are a gracious and compassionate God, slow to anger and abounding in love…" (Jonah 4:2). Jonah was not happy with God's love being poured out on his enemies, while Joseph couldn't wait to show God's love to those in a foreign culture whose people had him put into stocks.

So, how do I know if my suffering is the consequence of sin or part of God's unseen plan? There is not always an easy answer to such questions. When we sin, we might not see the consequences until years later, and it's not always easy to connect them to the wrong choice. Similarly, we know that God uses our obedience in ways we may never fully understand. God simply tells us to obey and to leave the results to Him. This may be why Hebrews 11 is divided in such a way as to show that the faith of many was rewarded with great victories, and others were rewarded by being "sawn asunder."

We must learn to accept that we may not be able to figure all this out. Perhaps this is why one of my favorite verses in Scripture is, "These all died in faith, not having received the promises, but having seen them afar off, and were persuaded of them, and embraced them, and confessed that they were strangers and pilgrims on this earth" (Hebrews 11:13 KJV). Having an eternal perspective doesn't answer all the tough questions, but it soothes the aching soul until we see Him face to face.

I JUST WANT TO BE ALONE

We often complain that we have no privacy. The kids get on our nerves. The boss needs the proposal tomorrow. Our spouse needs our time. The demands of people seem to be eating us alive. There are good reasons to get some time alone. We need time to decompress and just relax. We need time to recharge, reflect, and regroup. The desire to be alone should not always be interpreted as a rejection of others.

However, there can be bad reasons for wanting to be alone. When we're isolated, there's no one to hold us accountable. There is no responsibility in times of solitude. Jonah wanted to be alone and away from God, so he not only ran from God's command to go east but headed in the exact opposite direction and boarded a ship going west. Not only that, but he went down into the belly of the ship. He wanted privacy. He wanted to get away from anyone who might hold him accountable for his actions.

However, not only did God show up, but He brought Jonah to the upper deck for all to see. Many men surrounded Jonah, asking him all kinds of questions. He couldn't get any privacy. So here is the truth regarding the issue of privacy: There is no such thing. Psalm 139 makes it clear that wherever we go, He is there. Our so-called private thoughts are not private. Our secret sins are not really secret. What we look at on the computer late at night is not private.

We may not like this lack of privacy, but it's for our own good. When we truly fear God, it's because we understand that He is always with us. There is nowhere to hide. There is nowhere to run. Escape is not an option. So, allow this to be a warning. The next time you want to indulge in sinful behavior because you think you are alone, you are self-deceived. "Nothing in all creation is hidden from God's sight. Everything is uncovered and laid bare before the eyes of Him to whom we must give an account" (Hebrews 4:13). I just can't get any privacy—and that is a very good thing.

LOVE AS VIEWED BY THE RECIPIENT

"Love is patient, love is kind. It does not envy, it does not boast, it is not proud. It does not dishonor others, it is not self-seeking, it is not easily angered, it keeps no record of wrongs. Love does not delight in evil but rejoices with the truth. It always protects, always trusts, always hopes, always perseveres" (1 Corinthians 13:4-7).

LOVE IS PATIENT: Thank you for being patient with my shortcomings. It makes me feel accepted by you.

LOVE IS KIND: Your kindness is more than I could ever wish for, as it makes each day something to look forward to.

LOVE IS NOT ENVIOUS: I have never felt your envy toward me, which makes our relationship one of encouragement and not competition.

LOVE IS NOT BOASTFUL: You never speak arrogantly, which becomes an example for me to emulate.

LOVE IS NOT PROUD: Your humility affects the lives of those around you, and my life has been shaped by it.

LOVE IS NOT RUDE: There are no sharp edges in your speech or manners. I can express my thoughts without fear of attack.

LOVE IS NOT SELF-SEEKING: The fact that you are not self-seeking makes me feel important and not just tolerated.

LOVE IS NOT ANGRY: You never appear angry, which makes me feel safe and protected when I fall short.

LOVE DOES NOT KEEP SCORE: I have the freedom to fail without being reminded of past failures.

LOVE DELIGHTS NOT IN EVIL: Your avoidance of evil is a moral safeguard in our friendship.

LOVE REJOICES IN TRUTH: Your pursuit of truth gives me confidence that you are making wise decisions.

LOVE PROTECTS: I feel secure that you desire to protect my reputation, my emotions, and the hidden fears of my heart.

LOVE TRUSTS: Your consistent trust in me removes any suspicion and replaces it with trust in you.

LOVE GIVES HOPE: When you give hope to my life, I feel valued.

LOVE PERSEVERES: Your persevering love has been a faithful guide for my earthly pilgrimage.

YOUR LOVE HAS SET ME FREE.

IT'S NOT WHAT YOU SAY, BUT...

I suppose most of us, when we hear, "It's not *what* you say, but..." could fill in the blank with "...*how* you say it." That is a profound truth, and although not a Bible verse per se, it is certainly supported by Scripture. Consider such verses as "A gentle answer turns away wrath..." (Proverbs 15:1) or "Let your conversation be always full of grace, seasoned with salt" (Colossians 4:6). No doubt, we have all been on the receiving end of harsh words and have probably delivered some ourselves. Let me take a stab at going beneath the surface by looking at the words of Jesus when He said, "Out of the abundance of the heart, the mouth speaks" (Luke 6:46, Matthew 12:34).

In light of this, perhaps it's not *what* you say or even *how* you say it, but *why* you say it. Now, we are examining the motives behind what has been said. The why influences the what and the how. We say what we say out of the present condition of our hearts. "I can't believe you spent all that money without first asking me," a frustrated wife says to her husband. We know exactly what she said, and we know how she said it—but we don't know why she said it.

Let's look into this. Is her anger justified? Sure, she's angry because money is tight, and the purchase seemed unnecessary since she wasn't asked about it. She assumes her husband knows she would not have supported the purchase had she been asked. She assumes he tried to make this purchase by flying under the radar. She believes this shows a lack of trust. He is now feeling her disappointment and fires back, "I bought it because I knew you would say no because that's what you always say!"

Now, the argument escalates as the wife feels deceived, and the husband feels cheated. But suppose the wife saw the Visa bill and, without jumping to conclusions, sat down with her husband and asked him about the bill. She was gentle in her approach and not accusatory. He now feels the freedom to explain why he made the elaborate purchase. She responds by asking him if he really seems overly concerned about spending. He shares her feelings, which opens the door for an honest conversation.

So next time you enter any potential conflict, don't be too concerned about the what and the how, which is why I wrote this.

THE INVISIBLE JUNGLE

Whenever I take a jungle hike during my trips to the Amazon, I want Milton as my guide. Milton knows the jungle. It's an intimidating mass of foliage with unfamiliar plants and insects, all of which toy with your mind, making you think your next step may be your last. This foreboding landscape bares its teeth, and there is no welcome mat as you enter for one simple reason—you're not welcome. There is, however, comfort in knowing that Milton is leading the way.

There is a strange irony in all of this because we live in a far more threatening jungle than the one dressed in green. Yet, we trudge through it daily without consulting the guide. You would think that navigating in the dark would strike fear into our hearts, but often, we rely on our own instincts. The Word of God is "a lamp unto our feet and a light unto our path" (Psa. 119:105). It uses very graphic warning signals, such as don't be choked by the cares and riches of this life, or drowned in destruction for the love of money.

Any guide worth his salt will give careful instructions on the dangers of entering the jungles of Brazil. He knows the potential challenges. Those who have never been there before will listen carefully to his every instruction if they value their well-being. Yet this does not seem to translate when entering into the invisible jungle of spiritual darkness. There is less care for the soul: "What good is it for someone to gain the whole world, yet forfeit their soul?" (Mark 8:36).

What should be anticipated as a dangerous trek is seen as a walk in the park. People preparing for a trip into the jungle must bring the supplies they need to survive and weapons to protect themselves from danger. However, in the unseen jungle, the dangers of entertainment and worldly desires are seen as harmless fun. We plunge right in with the rest of the gullible crowd. Then, one day, we awaken to the reality that we have been deceived—but it's too late. The venom from the invisible jungle starts to do its work in the soul. It is slow yet relentless. Spiritual breathing becomes labored as the soul begins to atrophy. It won't be long before the toxin attacks the spiritual nervous system, and disorientation clouds all thought.

The ruler of this world turns out to have been our guide all along. He baited us with his winsome words, "Did God really say?" We bought into the lie, and now we have no idea where we are. That's the way of the jungle.

There is only one true guide, and His name is the Holy Spirit. He promises to lead us into all truth, even when we venture into the unseen dangers. He is actually better than Milton, and I find that hard to believe.

THE WAY OF THE FOOL

In Proverbs 7, we have the account of a foolish young man who is in the wrong part of town at the wrong time of night. The observer of this young man says he lacks judgment. A woman dressed like a harlot captures his eyes, and her seductive ways bring him into the realm of death.

We read this and smugly say to ourselves, "I've never done anything like that. I have never visited a prostitute or been taken captive by an immoral woman." Let's not be too hasty to dismiss this text as only addressing some wayward youth in a dark alley of city life. It actually addresses the lifestyle of many believers today. For you see, our technology now allows us to visit her home without ever leaving ours. The bright screen in our hands calls us to spend the evening entertained by something harmful. A few clicks online or a late-night Netflix binge, and we've acted foolishly. "So, if you think you are standing firm, be careful that you don't fall!" (1 Corinthians 10:12).

A MORAL CONTRADICTION

The following scenario is being played out daily across the nation. Pastor Jones, while out of town on a speaking engagement, purchases an inappropriate men's magazine. A member of his congregation on travel witnesses the purchase but remains quiet until he can privately meet with his pastor. The member lovingly confronts him. The pastor admits that he buys things like this several times a year when he's traveling. He and a church member decide to tell the church leaders about the issue, and the pastor is asked to step down for six months and seek help. Word gets out to the congregation, and to avoid more shame, the pastor moves away.

Meanwhile, a few miles away, Pastor Smith gives a culturally relevant illustration from a movie in his sermon. The congregation and spiritual leaders of the church applaud his ability to relate entertainment themes to real-life situations. His people are proud that he doesn't live a sheltered life but is in touch with the real world. The disturbing twist is that the illustrations were taken from movies that display nudity or have blatantly immoral themes.

What is the reason for this moral contradiction? The answer: cultural acceptance. If the world system accepts it, so does the church. What happens in the world also affects the church. This same thinking has made its way into Christian homes. Parents are shocked to find inappropriate material in their teens' internet history, but don't think twice about taking them to a movie that shows the same thing in public. It's confusing.

TAG LINES

I am painfully aware that most messages preached week after week evaporate from the minds of the congregation by the time they get home. I often forget what I say from week to week, so I try to sum up the whole sermon in one memorable idea. I call these "tag lines." I trust the following tag lines will bless you.

If we do not see ourselves as broken, we will never be able to relate or empathize with the brokenness of others.

If we only knew their story, we would have more sympathy than judgment.

Don't build your life around your children; build your life into your children.

When we are educated beyond our experience, it usually means we don't know what we are talking about.

Responding to guilt will never bring about conviction. Failing to respond to conviction will always evoke guilt.

Good preaching isn't about giving information but about sharing new understanding.

Good preaching takes people to where they don't want to go.

If you preach, make sure you're not just repeating what others have said. Commentaries can be helpful, but taking time to think deeply about yourself is the best way to learn.

The gospel is best communicated where the conviction of those who believe it can be observed by those who don't.

We must never underestimate the power of our conscience to convict us or to excuse us. The Word and the Spirit will rightly divide the two.

The fear of man often drives our decision-making. We either want to be liked or want to be seen as successful.

To the degree that we don't know Christ, we will trust in other things.

A person's constant craving for more will always be defeated by their inability to feel truly satisfied. This means that no matter how much someone wants or achieves, they will never feel fully content.

The world is temporally optimistic and eternally apathetic, while the church is to be eternally optimistic and temporally apathetic.

We often don't pray because we are not comfortable talking to a stranger.

The kingdom of God is anywhere the subjects of the kingdom believe that Jesus is King.

The law shows me where I need to be, but punishes me every time I try to get there. This means the law sets a standard, but I can never fully reach it without being judged for falling short of it.

I have a right relationship with grace and a right relationship with the law, because I have a right relationship with Christ, who kept the law on my behalf and graciously placed to my account the righteousness the law demands.

Leadership is the quality of life that encourages others to follow.

A good leader is tough, fair, and safe.

A leader's talent is about what they can do, while their character is about who they really are. It's important not to mix up these two because a person can be good at something but still lack strong character.

When we are obedient to what God has clearly revealed, God will often unfold what has not been revealed.

The ultimate irony is that the almighty dollar, which God advises us to trust the least, has the Person we are to trust the most written on it.

The unbeliever has adopted a belief, philosophy, or religion that tolerates and excuses their sin.

The immorality in entertainment that caused unbelievers to blush thirty years ago pales in comparison with what most believers openly endorse today.

Entering the wilderness is going anywhere emotionally, mentally, or physically where Christ is not our sufficiency.

Legalism is when someone follows the rules on the outside but fails to follow them on the inside.

Holiness is an inward spiritual response to God because of who I am in Christ.

Unity is the fruit of corporate humility.

The church is God's community, called out of spiritual darkness to enjoy the privilege of knowing God and making Him known.

The church should always be known more for the good it does than the evil it despises.

The tongue is the signature of the soul. The way we speak reflects what's in our hearts. What we say shows the true nature of our thoughts and feelings.

If my pride is injured, it means it's still very much alive.

Don't ask what Jesus would do. But what does Jesus think about what I am doing?

No nation has ever risen or fallen in its economy. Nations rise and fall on their morality, which dictates their economy.

Sin reproduces like rabbits, righteousness like oak trees. This means that bad actions can multiply easily, but good, righteous actions take time to develop and strengthen.

The world views Christ as a crutch in the Christian's life. How sad that we would portray any strength at all. He should be seen as a stretcher, for without Him, we can do nothing.

A midlife crisis can only happen to two types of people: those who are without eternal life and believers who have forgotten that eternal life has no midpoint.

Life is a vapor, no matter how long we live.

If life is a vapor, then so are the trials.

Contentment is coming to a place in my life where I desire nothing as opposed to coming to a place where I have everything.

A true witness is one whose life encourages those around him to speak of eternal matters.

Prosperity offers choices, and choices cause conflict, and conflict causes misery. McDonald's or Burger King.

What we think of as freedom to choose can sometimes trap us in the consequences of our decisions. This means that the more choices we have, the harder it can be to make the right ones, and the decisions we make can limit our true freedom.

Abraham was looking for a city whose builder and maker is God, while Lot was looking for a city whose builder and maker is man. Which city are we looking for?

Manipulation is arranging circumstances to make them appear as though they occurred naturally.

The manipulation of man will never trump the providence of God.

Keeping an arm's length from the world means we are moving in the direction of the world at what we perceive to be a safe distance, only to wake up tomorrow and find that we are living by the standards of the world today.

To read Scripture is to enter into the world of the unknown.

What we don't know about Scripture is infinitely greater than what we do know. Stay humble.

The Bible was not written to tell us what we can discover through our five human senses. It was written to tell us what our illuminated sixth sense discerns. This is called revelation.

As people belonging to heaven, we come from a place we've never physically been. This means that, although we live on Earth, our true home is in heaven, which we haven't experienced yet but are connected to spiritually.

The general revelation of His creation prepares the heart for the divine revelation of His Word.

There are five levels of revelation: Secret, hard to understand, not able to understand now, seen dimly, and that which is clear.

As we obey the Word of God, we are given new insight and a greater capacity to understand the insight.

Humility is believing that without Him, I can do nothing.

Jesus doesn't answer questions. He answers hearts.

A perfect heart is not a sinless heart. It is a heart that knows it is deceitful, invites God to inspect it, and daily repents of His findings.

Life is not fair because fairness is based on a temporal value system, while justice is based on an eternal value system.

Studying is like breaking open the seed of Scripture to understand it, while meditation is like turning it into something useful, like bread. This means that studying helps us learn the basic meaning, and meditation helps us apply it in a way that nourishes our lives.

Every marriage is programmed to fail. Energy must be put into the marriage to keep it alive.

Submission is an inner quality of gentleness in the wife that affirms the leadership of the husband within the limits of obedience to Christ.

A husband's leadership is an inner quality of courage that affirms his love for his wife by his willingness to die for her.

The American dream is a biblical nightmare. "For what shall it profit a man, if he shall gain the whole world, and lose his own soul?" (Mark 8:36, KJV).

Honesty might be limited, like someone cheating on their taxes but not on their spouse. Integrity, however, means being honest in every part of life. This shows that while honesty can sometimes be partial, integrity is about being truthful and consistent in all areas.

When a society loses its moral fiber, it redefines the terms of morality.

Drunkenness is "happy hour."

Adultery is "marital indiscretion."

Abortion is a "reproductive right."

Pornography is "adult entertainment."

There are three major storms in Scripture: the storm of discipline in Jonah's life, the testing storm of faith in the disciples' lives, and the storm that reveals believing faith before a lost world in Paul's life (revealed in Acts 27:13-44).

Materialism is enjoying the things of this world independently of glorifying God.

When knowledge is used the wrong way, it loses its value, which is why the world doesn't get better. This means that even though we have a lot of information, if it's misused or abused, it doesn't lead to positive change.

The condition of the world is the result of cumulative depravity.

The wisdom of the world improves life cosmetically. The gospel does not improve but makes something new.

People have always tended to reject any truth that limits their desires and replace it with a lie. This means that when truth challenges their actions or feelings, they often prefer to believe something false instead.

The church is to be a moral example, not a moral policeman.

Everyone leaves a wake in their life. What does yours look like?

Strong beliefs will always win over personal likes. Light will always defeat darkness. The truth will always defeat lies. Humility will always beat pride. This means that what is truly right and good will always overcome what is wrong or selfish.

The more you have, the harder it is to release it for the benefit of others. This is the law of inverse blessing.

The Word is more authoritative than signs, miracles, human reason, and experience.

In the parable of the Good Samaritan, the thieves wanted to get something for nothing. The priest and Levite were willing to get nothing for nothing. The innkeeper was willing to get something for something. The Samaritan was willing to give up everything for someone. That's Jesus.

Intelligence is the inherent ability to understand, while wisdom is the inherent ability to apply it.

Intellect sees life as it appears; wisdom sees life as it is.

Intelligence is knowing facts well, while wisdom is understanding the deeper truth behind those facts. This means intelligence is about gathering information, and wisdom is about understanding and applying that information in a meaningful way.

Intellect lives by the letter of the law; wisdom lives by the spirit of the law.

You can be a smart fool but never a wise one.

Wisdom does not guarantee you will have no problems in life. It simply guarantees you will not be the cause.

Since Satan is a liar and the prince of the world system, we can assume the world will lie to us at every turn.

No theology can explain God, for God is bigger than any system designed to explain Him.

When in conflict, always invite those who oppose you into your way of thinking rather than rebuking their way of thinking.

When bad things happen to others, we think it's because God is punishing them. When bad things happen to us, we believe it's because Satan is attacking us.

Joy is the inner confidence that God's grace will be sufficient to see me through my earthly pilgrimage.

Fun is a short-lived pleasure that comes from an event and disappears once it's over. This means that fun only lasts while the activity is happening, and once it ends, the feeling fades away.

We lie because we believe the benefits outweigh the consequences of telling the truth.

You can choose the food you eat and what your eyes behold, but not the words you hear.

Arguments rarely win arguments.

The godliest people I have known share these four characteristics: an insatiable appetite for the Word of God, a devoted prayer life, a care-free attitude about the things of this world, and a non-judgmental spirit toward those who are not as far along spiritually as they are.

During a conflict, you'll hear things that were never actually said, and you might say things you regret. This means that in heated moments, misunderstandings can happen, and emotions can lead to saying things you don't mean.

Anatomy of a conflict: Offense occurs; offense is shared with others; they take up offenses; sides form; past offenses unrelated to the original offense surface; suspicion on both sides develops; each side looks for evidence to confirm their suspicion; integrity is challenged; people call each other liars; and many are hurt.

In the midst of a conflict, third parties (no matter how well-intentioned) will never accurately report the facts from one offended party to the other.

When God miraculously provides, we should be more excited about who provided than the provision itself.

It's never good to match wits with a half-wit.

God has not called us to worship Him because He has a low self-image. He simply knows that He is all truth, and to worship anything else is humanism.

An excellent spirit is the ability to relate to God through the Spirit of God, achieved by obedience to the Word of God.

The Bible is amazing. Not because I know so much about it, but because it knows so much about me.

God has called us to financial freedom, not financial independence.

Grace is the unmerited favor of God upon man by which He saves man, protects him, teaches him, and empowers him to live the Christian life.

The real economic drain on any nation is sin.

Comparing evil with greater evil gives an excuse to sin (i.e., this movie is not as bad as most). The standard is Scripture, not the relative nature of evil.

Why should believers accept the findings of a depraved mind when we can trust the revealed truth of God's word?

How God speaks outside His Word: affliction, reproofs of life, natural laws, providential dealing, sowing/reaping, prayer, suffering, chastening, grace, and the leading of the Spirit.

Worship is our awareness of and reverent response to God's presence.

If we harbor bitterness toward someone who hurt us, we will hurt someone else unless we learn to see them as flawed and God as sovereign. Joseph saw how his brothers had hurt him, but he was not bitter because he saw God as having ordained the event.

The reality is, we don't always know the full truth. This means that sometimes we think we understand a situation, but we don't have all the facts or details.

Meditation is the mother of insight.

What was once called holiness is now referred to as legalism. It will soon be called relativism.

How could Jonah "flee from the presence of the Lord" when Psalm 139 says God is everywhere? We can never flee from His geographical presence, but we can flee from His moral will.

The Fullness Principle: Genesis 15:16 says that "the sin of the Amorites has not yet reached its full measure." So, is the iniquity of America almost full?

Faith is never a blind leap in the dark—that's foolishness. Faith in a person or object is always based on past experience with their reliability. Biblical faith is always based on divine revelation.

Scripture doesn't warn against what we are not likely to do.

Having the mind of Christ doesn't mean we know all He knows, but we think the way He thinks.

Jesus gives bad news to a good man in John 3 and good news to a bad woman in John 4.

In the parable of the prodigal son, the father gives good news to a bad son, which the good son sees as bad news.

In the parable of the Pharisee and tax collector, Jesus gives bad news to the law keeper and good news to the lawbreaker.

The inherent power of words is directly proportional to the relationship you have with the one who spoke them. "I hate you" from your father hurts far more deeply than "I hate you" from an acquaintance.

Jealousy causes us to throw javelins. Jealousy makes us attack others. This means that when we feel jealous, it can lead us to hurt people with our words or actions, just like throwing a spear to harm someone. Saul can tell you all about it.

Envy exposes my idols, which happen to be owned by someone else.

Those who take God seriously will take sin seriously.

Be a good steward of now and avoid being crushed by the weight of future consequences.

Keep a close eye on truth and a blind eye on error. Focus on the truth, and avoid spending too much time dwelling on mistakes. This means it's better to pay attention to what is right and good instead of always pointing out what is wrong.

If I meditate day and night while praying without ceasing, what time is left for work, sleep, family, and friends? In God's economy, all things are possible.

I'm thankful there is no debt ceiling on grace and even more thankful Congress isn't voting on it.

When life gets the best of you, just remember that Jesus got the best of life by conquering death.

Read, memorize, study, and meditate on God's Word. It nourishes the soul, enlightens the intellect, and imparts wisdom for living in a dying world.

Theology is often used to protect the gospel, but if not applied properly, it can destroy its simplicity. The gospel can defend itself.

Keep in mind that true forgiveness will cost you the right to get even. Remember, real forgiveness means giving up your right to seek revenge. This means that forgiving someone isn't just about saying it—it's about letting go of the desire to hurt them back.

In physical warfare, you can feel the pain. In spiritual warfare, the pain is numbed by pleasure, ease, and material possessions. The damage is far greater.

It is always better to humble ourselves before God than to be humbled by God. The latter is far more painful.

If you think you have lost your mind, it's next to your car keys, wherever they are.

Forgetting to remember and remembering to forget is driven by motive. What we choose to forget or remember depends on our reasons. This means that whether we let go of something or hold onto it often comes from what we want or feel in our hearts.

Anticipating what we think will make us happy can be a form of idolatry. Even when our expectations are realized, they rarely deliver what we anticipated.

The promises of God are not here. They are on the other side. "These all died in faith, not having received the promise" (Hebrews 11:13).

"Lord, I believe—help my unbelief" (Mk. 9:24) is the inner turmoil we all experience because our soul relates to the world, and our spirit relates to God. They are in conflict.

Criticism comes in two forms—an attack on our character or an attack on our ability. Be sure you know the difference when delivering a critique or being the recipient of one.

The world mocks what the Scriptures teach and daily experiences what they mock.

Our view of eternity guides our life of uncertainty.

Some people's spiritual maturity can't be quantified, while others can't be verified.

The reason we are called to be salt and light is that the world is rotting in darkness.

An illuminated mind is far superior to an unilluminated IQ.

Since Christianity is counter-cultural, make sure you are swimming upstream.

If we don't feel the current of the world, we must be drifting.

Scripture sees what God sees, which is not what we see. Therefore, ask Him to open your eyes so that you might behold wondrous things out of His law (Psalm 119:18).

Truth never changes lanes but always changes lives. Truth never changes its path, but it always changes the path of people. This means that truth remains constant and reliable, but only when we adhere to it.

How much evil would God have to remove before He would be considered good?

Poor management of time leads to an impoverished life.

If evolution is a positive trajectory, why are we declining so rapidly?

As long as there is pen and paper, "I forgot" is a poor excuse.

If you are teachable, you are reachable.

The more attached we become to this world, the more difficult life is when things don't work out as planned.

I love to hear from those who hear from God.

Living in the U.S. blinds us to how desperate we really are.

Love defines who we are, no matter where we are. Love shows who we really are, no matter where we go. This means that love is a part of our identity, and it shines through in our actions and choices, wherever we may be.

It is better to be on the right side of morality and the wrong side of history than to be on the right side of history and the wrong side of morality. Don't mess with God's standards.

The consequence of sin always outweighs its pleasure.

Expectations make us slaves to the improbable. Expectations can trap us into hoping for things that are unlikely to happen. This means that when we expect too much, we set ourselves up for disappointment because what we want may not be realistic.

Grace forgives but does not excuse.

When our work is not done with excellence, people assume we don't care or are incompetent.

If the church does not listen to the world and empathize with its suffering, the world will not listen to the church.

Distance and darkness never blind the eyes of an all-seeing God.

No matter how valid the argument, truth will always be suppressed by those who love darkness rather than light.

Studies show what we want studies to show.

The easiest way to make good choices is to stay away from bad ones. This means that avoiding mistakes from the start can help you make better decisions overall.

To study Scripture is to have Scripture study us.

Believing a lie paves the way for believing a bigger lie.

Memory is prejudiced, and it always sides with me.

It will never be the nature of man to encourage, but it will forever be his need to be encouraged.

Treasures today will be stuff tomorrow. That's why we have garage sales. What feels valuable today might just be clutter tomorrow. This means that things we treasure now might not stay important to us as time goes on.

Iron sharpening iron creates heat, and where there is heat, there is light. Rub shoulders with those you disagree with. You just might see the light.

There should be no human explanation for our lives.

Revelation without illumination is just information.

If you are not safe, your friends will be few.

Where love reigns, sin will be found wanting.

In Scripture, wherever God's name is conspicuously absent, His providence is conspicuously present: Esther.

Meditation yields Scripture's stubborn secrets.

We tend to hold on to grudges longer than we hold on to forgiveness.

We don't read the Bible so we can master it, but so that it can master us.

Our lives as believers should reflect a life fully devoted to God while living in a culture fully devoted to ignoring Him.

When we lack the facts, our counsel will be inadequate. This means that giving helpful guidance depends on knowing the truth about the situation.

We can't make people believe, but we can ask them why they don't.

Generosity is directly related to having an eternal perspective.

Money either binds me to this world or prepares me for the next. Money either keeps me focused on this world or helps me get ready for the next one. This means how we use money can either tie us to our current life or help us prepare for something greater in the future.

The love of stuff is the seed of greed.

God is not opposed to plans. He is opposed to being left out of the plans.

Any relationship fueled by pride is unsustainable.

Legacy is the imprint of character stamped on those who have observed our lives.

FIVE THEOLOGICAL BUCKETS

All of us know the Bible is a very complex book with tension, mystery, conundrums, paradoxes, parables, and various genres of writing. This naturally leads to various interpretations and some serious head-scratching.

Over the years, I have learned to put my thoughts into five buckets. In other words, when I come across a text, it will usually fall into one of five categories that I imagine as buckets.

Bucket number one: "The secret things belong to the lord (Deut. 29:29). The issue of where evil came from or why it continues to exist, I put in this bucket. Many times, I come across passages that fall into this category.

Bucket number two: "There are some things that are hard to understand (2Pet.3:15)." God ordering the slaughter of the Canaanites can be understood, but it is hard to understand.

Bucket number three: "We see through a glass dimly but then face to face (1 Cor.13)." Then there are those passages that we grasp but not as clearly as we would like. The parables we can understand, but are all nuanced, leaving us with an irritating pebble in the shoe.

Bucket number four: "I have more to tell you, but you are not able to receive it as of yet" (John 16:12-14). These are the words of Jesus to His disciples. This is an issue of maturity. An older, more mature saint may be able to grasp certain truths that a less seasoned veteran of the faith cannot handle.

Bucket number five: Rom. 1:20: "For since the creation of the world God's invisible qualities – his eternal power and divine nature – have been clearly seen, being understood from what has been made, so that people are without excuse." Atheists don't exist because God has made it clear about His existence. Simply put, God does not believe in atheists. We will be without excuse regarding that which is clear.

ADDICTED TO KNOWLEDGE AND ALLERGIC TO WISDOM

The following words were delivered by the Secretary General of the United Nations, U Thant, in the early 70s before 2500 people, including statesmen and scholars from around the world.

What element is lacking so that with all our skill and all our knowledge, we still find ourselves in the dark valley of discord and enmity? What is it that inhibits us from going forward together to enjoy the fruits of human endeavor and to reap the harvest of human experience? Why is it that, for all our professed ideals, our hopes, and our skills, peace on earth is still a distant objective seen only dimly through the storms and turmoils of our present difficulties?

The answer is quite simple. Humanism is focused on knowledge but avoids true wisdom. Pay attention to how we talk about skills, knowledge, human effort, experiences, and our beliefs. This means that humanism values information and achievement but often ignores deeper, wiser understanding. This is the tower of Babel lived out in the 20th and 21st centuries and will continue to be lived out as long as man sees himself as wiser than God.

We need to be clear about what we mean by this. Knowledge is collecting facts, while wisdom is knowing how to use those facts correctly. You can gather all the knowledge in the world, but without wisdom, you might end up in the same place you started. This means that just having information isn't enough—you need wisdom to make it truly useful. Just take a cold, hard look at the exponential increase in knowledge and a closer look at all the trouble the world is in. Why hasn't the knowledge solved our problems? In the 1700s, a pastor made the following observation. "Give me a candle and my bible, lock me in a dungeon, and I will tell you what the world is doing." Quite prophetic.

What worries me more isn't the lack of wisdom in the world. After all, we're told that Satan is a liar and has clouded the minds of those who don't believe. This means that people who don't believe are often misled and unable to see the truth clearly. My concern is with the church. We are addicted to theological knowledge and allergic to theological wisdom. In other words, we know but lack the wisdom in its application. Thus, the never-ending infighting.

This all came to a head a number of years ago when I was watching The Gospel Coalition and Together For The Gospel. I love hearing great scholars and preachers teach the deep things of God, but something came to my attention that caused me a great deal of consternation. There were six or seven men on stage answering big questions about robust theology. Thousands of people, both online and in person, were taking notes. But it occurred to me that these men couldn't start a church together. Why? Because they had too many differences in their beliefs. And now, wait for it, no two of them could plant a church.

I began thinking about the multiplication of churches around the Mediterranean rim, as recorded in the Book of Acts. Where were the creeds, statements of faith, and confessional views? Why did the church spread so rapidly without all the commentaries, blogs, websites, and doctrinal police scanning the internet looking for theological error that they can now expose to the nation?

Have we complicated the message? I believe we have. Hoping to write a book on this someday.

...BE WISE CONCERNING WHAT IS GOOD AND IGNORANT CONCERNING WHAT IS EVIL

"Everyone has heard about your obedience, so I rejoice because of you, but I want you to be wise about what is good and innocent about what is evil." Romans 16:19

This is a most interesting command coming from the apostle Paul. How does one stay ignorant about evil, seeing that we are immersed daily in evil that comes up on social media, music, the news, and a host of other platforms? There are some things you cannot avoid living in a fallen world. Martin Luther made a great statement. "You can't keep birds from flying over your head, but you can keep them from nesting in your hair." I think that says it all.

We don't need to be checking the news every ten seconds. We don't need to be on all social media platforms inundated with bad news and, often, sensual pictures. We already know what Jesus taught about this world.

"In this world, you will have tribulation. But be of good cheer! I have overcome the world." John 16:33b

When the US joined World War 2, we didn't know how it would end. But in the Bible, we already know the outcome. This is a big advantage because it helps guide us as we go through life each day, knowing the final result is a big advantage.

WISDOM IS A WEAPON

In the early stages of my Christian life, I came upon the following verse as recorded by Luke in the book of Acts. "But they could not stand up against the wisdom the Spirit gave him as he spoke" (Acts 6:10). You may recognize these words referring to Stephen, the first martyr.

The setting is Stephen standing before a self-appointed Jewish council. Note that Stephen was alone, dealing with a hostile group that wanted to kill him. But was he truly alone since the scriptures testify that he was full of God's grace, power, and wisdom? He clearly had the upper hand as these three gifts of grace conspired to destroy human arguments.

Let's listen in on another portion of scripture that gives further support to the power of wisdom. Jesus said to his disciples, "For I will give you words that none of your adversaries will be able to resist or contradict" (Lk. 21:15).

At the end of the Sermon On The Mount, we read "For he taught them as one having authority, and not as the scribes" (Matt. 7:29). Then in John (7:45-47) we read this,

"Finally, the temple guards went back to the chief priests and the Pharisees, who asked them, 'Why didn't you bring him in? No one ever spoke the way this man does, the guards replied.'"

There seems to be a theme where wisdom wins the day. Why is that? Because people know what wisdom looks like when they are face-to-face with it. They don't know how to counter it, even though they know it's true. This is why believers must know the word in order to counter the vacuous arguments of the world.

For it is written:

"I will destroy the wisdom of the wise; the intelligence of the intelligent I will frustrate. Where is the wise person? Where is the teacher of the law? Where is the philosopher of this age? Has not God made foolish the wisdom of the world?" (1Cor.1:19-20)

"But he who fails to find me injures himself; all who hate me love death" (Prov. 8:36)."

THE BINARY GOSPEL

The term binary is not a new one, but has made its way into our everyday vocabulary thanks to computer technology. Here is how the word is defined by the Oxford Dictionary: "Relating to, composed of, or involving two things."

Much of life is binary: two things paired together in a way that brings contrast. Focus and clarity, up or down, East or West, black or white, in or out, active or passive, true or false— they are all binary.

The beauty of binary is that there's no confusion. Everything is clear and simple. In binary code, a one is never a zero, and a zero is never a one. This means there's no room for misunderstanding or doubt— everything is either one thing or the other. This binary nature shows the clarity of the true Gospel in contrast to religion, which clouds the issue regarding eternal life. While religion blurs the edges, the binary Gospel brings eternity into sharp focus. Here are a few binary statements made in scripture about the Gospel.

"Very truly I tell you, whoever hears my word and believes him who sent me has eternal life and will not be judged but has crossed over from death to life." John 5:24

Here, you have two binary opposites. You have either passed from death into life, or you haven't.

"Whoever has the Son has life; whoever does not have the Son of God does not have life. I write these things to you who believe in the name of the Son of God so that you may know that you have eternal life." 1 John 5:12-13

Binary again. You either have life in the son, or you don't. You either know you have eternal life, or you don't.

"For he has rescued us from the dominion of darkness and brought us into the kingdom of the Son he loves, in whom we have redemption, the forgiveness of sins." Col.1:13-14

You have been rescued, or you haven't. You are in the Kingdom, or you are not.

"Jesus replied, "Very truly I tell you, no one can see the kingdom of God unless they are born again." John 3:3

You are either born again or you are not.

"Therefore, since we have been justified through faith, we have peace with God through our Lord Jesus Christ." Rom. 5:1

You either have peace with God, or you don't.

All the prophets testify about Him that through His name, everyone who believes in Him will receive forgiveness of sins." Acts 10:43

You have either been forgiven or you haven't.

"Therefore, there is now no condemnation for those who are in Christ Jesus." Rom. 8:1

You are either condemned or you are not.

"For the Son of Man came to seek and save that which was lost." Luke 19:10

You are either lost or found.

"For it is by grace you have been saved, through faith—and this is not from yourselves, it is the gift of God, not by works, so that no one can boast." Eph. 2:8-9

You are saved by faith, or you are not. It is a gift, or it is by works. It cannot be both.

I could keep going, but I think you see my point. The default mode of the human heart is to blur the lines, and the lines will always be blurred when human effort or good works are involved. Note how fuzzy things get if we were to take any of the above verses and add the haze of religious self-effort to them.

"For it is by grace you have been saved as long as you go to church and occasionally drop a twenty in the offering plate."

"I tell you the truth, no one can see the kingdom of God unless he tries real hard to keep the Golden Rule."

Is it grace or good works that save me? And how hard do I have to try to keep the Golden Rule?

I often wonder at the heart of man that he feels such a need to help God out by adding to the clarity of His word and work. When Jesus said, "It is finished" at the cross, why do we think we need to add a few finishing touches? Would we try to improve a Rembrandt? And if we did, do we really believe it would enhance the masterpiece? The question is rhetorical, but the answer is not: Christ has already done it all on my behalf. What could I possibly add to it?

So, if you find yourself struggling with eternity based on your religious performance, just remember this: God did not send His Son to leave us confused about our eternal destiny. You are either condemned or you are not. You're either in the kingdom or you're out of it. You are saved by grace through faith, or you are not. You either have the life in the Son, or you don't. While religion may often obscure the clear message of the Gospel, the Scriptures are clear: it's all of Jesus or none of Him. It's a zero, or it's a one. We can always know where we stand, not because of us, but because of Him. It's binary.

MORE BROKEN THAN WE THINK

Believers desire clarity in their doctrine, ethics, and moral outlook from a biblical perspective. Certainly, a worthy endeavor. But in this lifelong pursuit, we run into many speed bumps as well as roadblocks. The Bible simply doesn't lend itself to a clear hermeneutic (the science of interpretation) as much as we would like it to.

This is not to imply there is no clarity at all. Salvation by grace through faith in Christ alone is clear. The bodily resurrection of Jesus from the grave is clear. Marriage between a man and a woman is clear. I could go on about that which is clear. However, the rest of the book remains silent or vague on many issues that lead to church splits and various other problems.

The fact that we are broken, though redeemed, does not make everything clear. In a fallen world, it is virtually impossible to understand the full revelation of God's infallible truth. Brokenness means just that. Your part of brokenness sees scripture through a different lens than mine. This is where we show grace and humility. When that time arrives, we will feel more united than ever. By practicing kindness and humility, we will unite in a way that is more resilient and peaceful than before.

THE CULTURAL NARRATIVE

Whoever controls the narrative controls the culture. One of the greatest marketing strategies ever devised by man has been well executed by those who combine the words progressive and hate. Progressive has such a positive ring to it. Who wants to be regressive and live in the past?

Hate is used against those who don't agree with progress, especially regarding the changes in views on sexuality. Here are some thoughts on how the forces of evil work under their leader. This suggests that individuals who oppose specific changes, such as those concerning sexual perspectives, might encounter hate or criticism. The discussion here focuses on how these negative forces function.

Since Jesus refers to Satan as the ruler of this present age, we must expect the lost world of humanity to promote darkness. Even if we had only the teachings of Jesus to go by, it would not be too hard to anticipate the enemy's strategy.

The first order of business would be to destroy the very fabric of society by annihilating the family. Make divorce easy and painless. Separate families at mealtime by having each member addicted to entertainment, grab their food, and retreat to separate rooms.

Then, redefine marriage by erasing gender from one man and one woman to anyone you choose. Redefine gender from male and female to endless classifications. Make each classification fluid so people can be whatever they want to be from day to day.

The next step is to break down all sexual boundaries and start a sexual revolution. The goal is to confuse young people early on, making them unsure of their sexual identity. This involves encouraging younger generations to question and feel uncertain about their sexuality, which makes it more difficult for them to understand or define themselves.

Invent pronouns for identification so as to disrupt society and bring about unsustainable communication with hefty lawsuits in tow. Watch the anger reach a boiling point at school board meetings and congressional hearings.

Then, move into a culture of death by redefining life. A child in the womb is no longer a person but a choice. Rearrange terminology and move the Trojan Horse into the marketplace by cleverly reversing the meaning of words and phrases.

Planned Parenthood sounds like an organization that helps people become parents, but in reality, it aims to end the life of the very child who would make you a parent. This means the name implies one thing—helping people with parenthood—but its actions aim to stop pregnancies, which prevents people from becoming parents.

A woman has the right to do what she wants with her own body: No argument there. Tone it, tattoo it, and tan it. However, a peek under the covers of such subliminal rhetoric reveals we are not talking about her body but another body made in the image and likeness of God.

Reproductive rights: Sounds like a desire to reproduce, when it is just the opposite.

Reproductive health care: Who doesn't want that for all people? Yet below the surface, the health care of the child is removed.

To maintain the momentum of confusion, the enemy moves into other arenas. Keeping people in darkness comes by offering alternative gods. The god of pleasure, power, education, technology, politics, amusement, sex, and a host of other deities. These gods conspire together by dangling the carrot of utopia with the promise that it's just over the horizon, and the next technological advancement will usher it in.

To complete the progressive narrative, there must be a means of promoting it to society; this is accomplished by liberalizing the government and the educational system with the express purpose of capturing the minds of young people and then repeating the narrative over and over and over until it is hardwired in the minds of an entire generation. This keeps the culture off-balance and confused.

"Keep your laws off my body" means not wanting others to control what happens to your body. Here again, the rhetoric fails to talk about the body of the child. But this should also apply to laws that protect you from being hurt or killed, especially when you're vulnerable and can't defend yourself. This means wanting freedom over your body but also recognizing the need for laws that protect your life from harm. Such smokescreens, over time, cloud the issue, and such indoctrination will soon blind an entire nation to the truth...

Now it is time to move in for the kill through intimidation by calling anyone who disagrees with this agenda a narrow-minded, intolerant, hateful bigot on the wrong side of history.

Checkmate. Or is it? Those who control the narrative control the culture. Yet we are called to love those who hate us and do good to those who persecute us. We are called to be salt and light in a culture sinking into darkness. This isn't just a marketing strategy, but the eternal power of the gospel of grace through which the church influences the culture.

ENTROPY AFFECTS THE CHURCH AS WELL AS THE NATURAL WORLD

I know what you are thinking. What is entropy? If you studied science or engineering, this term is very familiar, but if English or political science was your major, this may be a rather esoteric term. You can Google esoteric.

Entropy describes the randomness, decay, or uncertainty of natural order. A building left to itself will decay over the years. Energy must be invested to keep it from collapsing. If we go back and look at the Book of Acts, we see the church exploding. Answers to prayer and healing are sprinkled throughout the book. But look at the church today. It is hardly recognizable if we compare it with the Book of Acts. What happened?

The typical answer is that the miraculous drifted away after the canon of scripture was closed or when the last apostle died. There are valid reasons to consider this approach. However, it is a more subjective interpretation and lacks the clarity of a more objective one.

Just to let you know where I am coming from, I am not Charismatic or Pentecostal, but I have known many who live victorious lives based on their theology. The apostle Paul looked at a crippled man and "saw that he had faith to be healed." Did faith to be healed pass away? Since when has faith been subject to the law of entropy?

I have always been a questioner. I don't like canned answers. I doubt you do, either.

FAITH: A BLIND LEAP IN THE DARK?

Faith is often misunderstood because of how people use the word, especially believers. When we tell our non-believing friends that they need to have faith, they might think it means taking a blind leap without knowing where they're going. This means that "faith" is sometimes seen as believing in something without any evidence or certainty, which is not the true meaning. We must be able to present what we believe more cogently than some mystical view of God and the gospel.

If I am approached by a stranger in New York City who wants to borrow $100 and promises to mail $100 after he gets paid in two weeks, and I give it to him, that is a blind leap of foolishness. If it's a good friend who wants to borrow the money, that's a different situation. I know they can be trusted, so I don't worry about the loan. It's given with trust and confidence. This means that when you trust someone completely, you feel secure lending them money, believing they'll pay it back.

My trust in him comes from my past experiences with his character. You can have faith in a watch that always tells the correct time or in your old Jeep that always starts on a cold morning. This means that faith is based on previous experiences and trustworthiness, whether it's with a person or something like a trusted object that demonstrates itself over time.

FINISHING WELL

As I was preparing for my retirement at Reston Bible Church after 47 years, someone said to me, "We want you to finish well." I started asking myself, What does finishing well look like? This was a haunting question that caused me much pondering. Where in scripture does it define finishing well?

I think the Apostle Paul gives us some insight when he says, "I have fought the good fight, I have finished the race, I have kept the faith" (11 Tim 4:7). Note the three expressions, "I have fought the good fight." This tells us he saw the Christian life as a war zone and not a playground. "I have finished the race." His time was up, and he could look back with a sense of fulfillment empowered by God's grace. "I have kept the faith." He never wavered as he looked back over the hardships and trials.

Here is what I take away from this text. He had few regrets and a clear conscience. That is what finishing well looks like, but we must prepare for this in our daily walk. If you are young, you have an advantage in finishing well. Now is the time to take inventory because life is brief, and eternity is long; invest heavily in the latter.

HAVE YOU BEEN SCAMMED?

With the internet in full force, even the best have been scammed or at least drawn into one. Being on the elderly side and probably the least qualified person to sit behind a computer, I'm an easy target. All my children are in their forties and can get a bit upset when I get hustled. "Dad, call us before you step into an ad or email that is a bit suspicious."

My problem is that I don't know what is suspicious. Many years ago, when there were no home computers and no internet, my wife and I got a postcard in the mail congratulating us on the birth of our first child. The card read something like this: "Congratulations on the birth of your first child." These places get their info from the hospital, thus the arrival of our card. "You are a winner." Surprise, surprise, aren't we all? It went on to tell us that if we came to their store, we would be the winner of one of the following prizes. A car seat, a highchair, a bassinet, a stroller, or the grand prize: five 8x10 photographs captured by the renowned Harris & Ewing studios in Washington, D.C., known for photographing presidents.

I may be dumb, but I'm not stupid. Halfway there, in our blue station wagon, I turned to my wife and said, "I was born on a Friday but not last Friday." Doubt I really said that, but something to that effect.

How can any company afford to give away an expensive tangible prize to the parents of every newborn in Fairfax County, Virginia? The answer: they can't. They would be out of business before they opened. It soon dawned on me that the only prize that would cost them nothing was the pictures. I turned to Kay and said that every parent would get the grand prize. Did they? Oh yeah! Upon entering, you drew a number from a big glass bowl. I stood around to see if anyone got a crib or a car seat. You guessed it. No, not one. Nada, zilch. The pictures cost the store nothing. You had to drive downtown, pay for parking, and purchase extra for the grandparents. Then drive home and come back a week later to pick up the photos.

This was, in fact, a scam. Many scams are legal because what they say is literally true with a hitch. In this scenario, the hitch was the pictures. Thus, the store didn't technically lie but was misleading.

About a year ago, I was on my computer doing some writing when, out of nowhere, my screen shut down and popped up a warning. "Your computer has been hacked. Call Apple at the number on your screen immediately." I made the call and was told, "Your computer is being used to sell child pornography." Did I say to myself, "What an obvious scam! These guys are amateurs."

No! I called 911 and said I'm having a heart attack. Will the Feds get to me before the ambulance does?

Okay, okay, I'm given to exaggeration from time to time. I was not about to call anyone except the number on the screen. I ended up calling and was told that this issue is so serious that I am not to talk to no one, including my wife, or it would interfere and compromise the Federal Trade Commission's Investigation. The man on the line said he was transferring me to the FTC. For three days, I was given special instructions to talk only to my agent. He sent me a pic with his name and badge #. I was really impressed. My agent was even more impressed at what a sucker I was.

On the third day, I decided to call the FTC. Guess what. They contact you through the mail and not the phone if they suspect suspicious behavior. Okay, I have let you in on my vulnerability and gullibility.

Here is a one-question quiz to see if you have been scammed regarding the greatest issue in the world: eternal life. Here is the question asked by the Philippian jailor… "Sirs, what must I do to be saved?" (Acts 16:30). And Paul and Silas responded with, "Believe in the Lord Jesus, and you will be saved- you and your household" (Acts 16:31). Religion would have responded with "Believe in the Lord Jesus and keep the commandments and always do your best and God might let you in."

Let's look into this. Here are some really hard sayings about the human condition. Very offensive.

"Then Noah built an altar to the Lord and, taking some of all the clean animals and clean birds, he sacrificed burnt offerings on it. The Lord smelled the pleasing aroma and said in his heart, "Never again will I curse the ground because of humans, even though every inclination of the human heart is evil from childhood. And never again will I destroy all living creatures, as I have done" (Genesis 8:20-21).

"The heart is deceitful above all things, and beyond cure. Who can understand it?" (Jeremiah 17:9). You have been taken for a ride and embraced the greatest eternal scam by believing you will enter heaven through your own good works. Accept what Paul said to the jailor, and you will be saved.

IN LIGHT OF ETERNITY

Time is relentless. With its calendars and clocks, deadlines and datelines, who can ignore this daunting giant? It never rests, never tires, and boldly reminds me that I'm falling behind. I wish I could boycott all expressions bearing his name..." wait a minute," "just a second," "from time to time," and "year in and year out."

Scripture calls *time out* on this minute muncher. No longer must we view time as a measuring stick inexorably winding its way through history. This temporal beast is brought to its knees in light of eternity. Consider the following, "for a thousand years in thy sight are but as yesterday when it is past, and as a watch in the night" (Psa. 90:4); For this corruptible must put on incorruption, and this mortal must put on immortality" (1Cor.15:53); "For our light affliction, which is but for a moment worketh for us a far more exceeding and eternal weight of glory" (11 Cor. 4:17); Whereas ye know not what shall be on the morrow. For what is your life? It is even a vapor, that appeareth for a little time and then vanished away" (James 4:14); "And the world passeth away and the lust thereof: but he that doth the will of God abideth forever" (1John 2:17).

God, as the above verses give witness, consistently places the temporal next to the eternal. The purpose seems obvious. Time is only a measuring device for the here and now. Eternity is what really counts. When the last grain of sand passes through the hourglass, it will mark the end of time and usher in the beginning of eternity. What will history record but the futility of man's wisdom? Will it really matter how many Big Macs were sold? Will the heavens shake if the Titans don't make it into the playoffs? Will anyone really care how the Dow Jones Industrials closed out on that final day? "But the day of the Lord will come as a thief in the night; in which the heavens shall pass away with a great noise, and the elements shall melt with fervent heat, the earth also and the works that are therein shall be burned up" (11 Pet. 3:10).

I have no desire to mock time. It holds value, but only when viewed through the lens of eternal purposes. The believer is called to be indifferent to the temporary and hopeful about the eternal, whereas the unbeliever remains indifferent to the eternal and focuses on the temporary.

IS THIS THE REAL WORLD?

I can imagine what the reader is thinking. Is this going to be one of those mystical Twilight Zone articles where I try and prove we don't really exist? All that we experience is just an illusion. No, there are plenty of those bazaar posts all over social media, and they have been around for decades.

I believe the biblical narrative tells us we are not in the real world. The world we are in is real, but it is not the real world for one simple reason. We detect all of reality through our five human senses, which are fallen and lack what Adam and Eve experienced in an innocent environment. Try and imagine all of your senses detecting everything perfectly. That would be true reality. And in the New Heavens and the New Earth, we will perceive all things perfectly.

How do we know what a perfect life is like where the senses have never been affected by the Fall?

Jesus is the only true human. He does not have a fallen nature. He is perfectly righteous. He is without sin. He is God incarnate. In His humanity, he feels what we feel and relates to our pain and suffering. In His deity, he knows all and shows what reality looks like if you see life through His lens. Jesus said to Pilot, "My kingdom is not of this world" (John 18:36). His kingdom has always been an upside-down kingdom, which shows us what reality really looks like. We serve to lead, we give to get, we humble ourselves to be exalted, we die to live, we lose our lives to find it. Jesus lived in true reality. There was no pretense. No hypocrisy. No falsehood. We cannot say that about ourselves. "Let God be true but every man a liar" (Romans 3:4).

When we enter the New Heaven and the New Earth, we will encounter true reality. It will be an awe-inspiring experience. Our flawed human senses will function flawlessly, and only then will we fully experience true reality. In the meantime, we can rest in such assurance.

MANIPULATION

We have all employed this word when we feel taken advantage of. "My competitor took full advantage of me through diabolical means of manipulation." We put the pieces together and saw how we were sucker punched. So, what exactly is manipulation? Manipulation is arranging circumstances in such a way that they appear to have occurred naturally. Manipulation is not always executed with bad motives. Let's say you want Sally and George to meet, so you arrange for them to have tickets to a sporting event where they just happen to have adjoining seats. It's still manipulation, even if a good motive drives the purpose. Manipulation questions God's providence. Providence is God's power to take the good, the bad, and the ugly of human responsibility and bring about His sovereign plan.

The ultimate manipulation in scripture is the narrative of Isaac, Rebekah, Jacob, and Esau. The Lord told Rebekah that Esau, the elder, would serve Jacob, the younger. God's word cannot be broken. Jacob was called by the Lord from time in eternity past to be the next patriarch. But Rebekah felt she needed to help God out by having Jacob steal the patriarchal blessing from Esau by serving Isaac his favorite food before Esau could prepare his. There was no need to make circumstances seem as if they occurred naturally. God's plan cannot be hindered by human manipulation.

Abraham's lie about Sarah being his sister was pointless manipulation because Isaac had not yet been born, and he was the promised seed. An atomic bomb could not have destroyed Abraham before Isaac's birth. Both of these manipulative schemes caused untold pain but, in God's providence, brought forth the promised Messiah. Amazing! So, I guess it is a good thing after all to manipulate? May it never be! It is never right to do wrong so that good will come.

God accomplishes His will, but we bear the consequences of not trusting Him. So, let's honestly evaluate our tendencies toward manipulation. Consider what aspects you may be attempting to control in your family, workplace, church, or friendships. Manipulation is a blatant lack of faith for which we hang ourselves. Jacob had to leave home because of manipulation. Pharaoh rebuked Abraham for lying about Sarah. We never need to help God out when we know the truth of His word. Sorry for trying to manipulate you into obeying God.

LIFE IS A MIRAGE

A mirage differs from a hallucination. It is an optical phenomenon caused by the refraction of light through a layer of hot air near the ground, producing a misleading image of something that doesn't exist. On the other hand, a hallucination is a sensory perception of something that does not exist, often caused by a disorder in the nervous system or the mind. A mirage is not an illusion or a hallucination because it is a real physical effect that can be captured on camera," even though it doesn't exist.

Many stories have been related about people lost in the desert or wilderness who see water or an oasis. I use this to describe our fallen world. I'm not suggesting that what we experience isn't real. The experience is just as real as the thirsty wanderer looking for water and seeing it just a few hundred yards ahead, but when he arrives, it disappears. It was simply a mirage.

The book of Ecclesiastes captures this so well. The writer, most likely Solomon, takes us on a roller coaster ride. He keeps the reader off guard throughout the book. His never-ending refrain that "vanity of vanities, all is vanity" is the main theme of the book (Eccl 1:3a). Vanity is simply another expression for mirage or smoke.

Life without Jesus is a mirage. Lost humanity keeps seeing the future of technology solving our problems, or a new medicine or philosophy of life that will usher in utopia. But once these advances arrive, they come with unanticipated problems. Cars and planes produce toxic exhaust, new medications have severe side effects, the faster the computer, the longer we are at the office, and the very problem computers were designed to solve. We can't seem to extricate ourselves from this fallen world.

You see, the Fall is the very reason we can't escape. We are trapped in a closed system, and there is no way out. Just as we start seeing the utopia we have been dreaming of, the bottom falls out. Ecclesiastes says in its endless refrain, "Meaningless! Meaningless!" Says the teacher, "Utterly meaningless! Everything is meaningless" (Eccl.1:2). "Whoever loves money never has enough: whoever loves wealth is never satisfied with his income. This, too, is meaningless" (Eccl. 5:10). In other words, the heat waves of wealth create a distant view of what money can do for you, but once you have it, the mirage spoils the day.

Here is another example from Solomon.

"I denied myself nothing my eyes desired; I refused my heart no pleasure.

My heart took delight in all my labor, and this was the reward for all my toil.

Yet, when I surveyed all that my hands had done and what I had toiled to achieve, everything was meaningless, a chasing after the wind; nothing was gained under the sun" (Eccl. 2:10-11).

Here, the writer portrays life under the sun as a mirage. Life under the sun is an expression of life without God. It is a man roaming about this globe trying to find or create a utopia. It can be a sexual pursuit, a materialistic pursuit, or an emotional high. You can clearly see it in the distance, but once you get close, it evaporates. Our fallen nature causes these heat waves, which seem to paint a beautiful picture of utopia, but once we reach it, we realize it's all meaningless.

Tom Brady, after his fourth or fifth Super Bowl win, began to ask the question, "Is this it?" Now he has seven rings, but it wasn't enough. It was a mirage. This forced him to decide between his family and another ring. The ring was a mirage, but the divorce was a reality.

Who are the most attractive, rich, and talented people in the world? Movie stars, hands down. They have it all. I wonder what the divorce rate in Hollywood is. I know it is way above the national average. Apparently, wealth, good looks, and talent fade rapidly once all three are experienced.

So, where does this first show up?

Now, the serpent was craftier than any of the wild animals the Lord God had made. He said to the woman, "Did God really say, 'You must not eat from any tree in the garden'?" The woman said to the serpent, "We may eat fruit from the trees in the garden, but God did say,

'You must not eat fruit from the tree that is in the middle of the garden, and you must not touch it, or you will die.'"

"You will not certainly die," the serpent said to the woman. "For God knows that when you eat from it your eyes will be opened, and you will be like God, knowing good and evil." (Genesis 3:1-24)

Did you catch the mirage? You will be like God. In one sense, they would, but not in the way Satan intended it. The mirage through a piece of fruit produced death. The mirage is nothing more than bait with a hook inside. A lure, if you will.

The lottery has turned out to be one of the greatest mirages of all. Advertising creates its own illusion. And where does all the stuff end up? In the trash or at a garage sale.

The greatest mirage of all is the computer, which I happen to be using to write this. Everyone was supposed to get home earlier from the office because computers were doing all the work. Unfortunately, your competition also uses computers, so yours had better be faster. Stay a little longer at the office to make up for the difference.

Developing an eternal perspective will help erase the mirage. Heaven is more real than this present world.

PILGRIM

"All these people were still living by faith when they died. They did not receive the things promised; they only saw them and welcomed them from a distance, admitting that they were foreigners and strangers on earth." (Hebrews 11:13).

Pilgrim has sort of a homespun ring to it, don't you think? You know, pumpkin pie, hot apple cider, Thanksgiving, and the Mayflower. The word may conjure up cozy thoughts, but it seems God had a different purpose when he planted it in scripture. It is assigned to those who are looking for a city that has foundations whose builder and maker is God (Hebrews 11:10).

Reflect on this expression for a while, and you'll find that "pilgrim" becomes a trusted companion on this journey we call life. A bit of a nuisance, but nevertheless, a friend in time of need. Just when you settle down in the easy chair of the world and its ways, this noisy noun climbs off the pages of scripture and sings a few bars of "this world is not my home."

Here are seven pesky letters that won't mind their own business. If you don't believe me, just spend a few minutes in Hebrews 11:13, where the great saints of the past confessed that they were strangers and pilgrims on the earth. Now stroll through the Galleria and see if this two-syllable giant doesn't spoil your day. Unannounced and uninvited, the pilgrim appears on the horizon of your conscience, poised and ready to do his thing. Convict! Nothing shy about old pilgrim.

You can feel him breathing down your neck and eyeballing your every thought. As the world parades its goodies before you, the pilgrim whispers sweet nothings in your ear, "For you brought nothing into this world, and it is certain we will carry nothing out (1 Timothy 4:7). Killjoy!

You begin to wish you had never heard of this guy, much less been called one. You try desperately to dodge this intruder, but it's no use; he has the bases covered. You try to regroup while remaining calm as you plan your next strategy. "How can I put a lid on pilgrim?" you ask. The world offers a ready answer. "Indulge!" is the cry echoing from the chambers of materialism and entertainment.

Certainly, such a distraction will put the muzzle on this merchant of holiness, but he is much too clever for such an anemic ploy, just as you focus on some must-have item, who should appear with a script in hand, but a pilgrim. "Do you really need that?"

He inquires. "Can you afford it?"

"Will it glorify God?"

Don't you just despise his practicality at a time like this? You're quick, however, with your own defense, and your ability to rationalize peaks when conviction enters the scene. "But everyone else owns one, why can't I?" "I'll just close my eyes during the dirty part of the film." "What's wrong with a little worldly entertainment anyway?" Undaunted and not easily discouraged, the pilgrim strikes back. "Love not the world, nor the things that are in the world (1 John 2:15)."

Does a pilgrim have no room for enjoyment? Is this Eeyore in spiritual clothing? Absolutely not, for the pilgrim reminds us of the words from the apostle Paul, who said, "Command those who are rich in this present world not to be arrogant nor to put their hope in wealth, which is so uncertain, but to put their hope in God, who richly provides us with everything for our enjoyment" (1 Tim. 6:17).

You're down for the count, and mentally, you're beginning to hemorrhage. Time to call it quits. You're home now, and a quick inventory of the day's activities registers victory. A smile begins to work its way across your face as you rehearse the would-be disaster had pilgrim not held your hand. You didn't fall for the temporal value system of the world. You didn't get sucked into some worthless form of entertainment that would have etched its mark upon your soul. You were, in fact, able to hang tough because of a loyal companion named Pilgrim.

Abraham was a pilgrim, and since we are children of Abraham through faith in Christ, guess what that makes us? Sure, it's hard. It was hard for Abraham as well. I suspect, however, he never strolled through the Galleria.

REVELATION: ENTERING THE WORLD OF THE UNKNOWN

1. **We would never know** where the world and the universe came from. However, the scripture tells us in no uncertain terms.

"In the beginning": That's Time

"God created": That's Energy

"The heavens": That's Space

"And the earth": That's Matter

There it is, the total of everything as science explains it: time, energy, space, and matter. Meanwhile, NASA is spending billions to discover where the universe came from. By the way, space flights carry an expensive payload, while the Bible app is free to download. As a disclaimer, I love what NASA is doing, except when it spends my money searching for answers about where the universe came from, and other such things—answers that are readily available in the holy scriptures.

2. **We would never know** why we are here to enjoy God and glorify him forever.

3. **We would never know** why education without wisdom is a dead-end street. Remove the wisdom, and you have a snake trying to shuffle cards. This is proven daily in all schools of higher education. Remove the wisdom of scripture, and life dies a slow death. Just read today's news or tomorrow's; it's all the same.

4. **We would never know** the heart is incurably wicked (Jer. 17:9)

5. **We would never know** there are two kingdoms at war with one another.

6. **We would never know** we have an enemy.

7. **We would never know** about the world, the flesh, and the devil.

8. **We would never know** why a man can't seem to fix his problems.

9. **We would never know** that man is the problem, and when the problem tries to solve the problem, *that's a problem.*

10. **We would never know** the nature of sin and its consequences.

11. **We would never know** that the wisdom of man is foolishness with God (1 Cor 2).

12. **We would never know** there is a heaven and hell.

13. **We would never know** how to enter the kingdom of God.

14. **We would never know** man's inability to get along with his fellow man.

15. **We would never know** why there are wars and rumors of wars.

16. **We would never know** how to have peace in the midst of conflict.

17. **We would never know** the divine blueprint for marriage or what marriage represents.

18. **We would never know** the value of life.

19. **We would never know** why a man can't control his passions.

20. **We would never know** that God is sovereign, omniscient, omnipresent, and omnipotent, and that all things work together for good, to those who love God and are called according to His purpose (Rom 8:28).

21. **We would never know** that He is coming again to usher in the New Heavens and the New Earth.

22. **We would never know** that what we don't know is infinitely more than what we do know. That should humble us to the core.

23. **We would never know** that salvation is a gift from God and cannot be earned through good works.

24. **We would never know** what it means to be born again.

25. **We would never** know the kingdom of God is upside-down living.

26. **We would never** know the difference between wisdom and knowledge.

27. **We would never** know that this is not the real world but a distorted image of the one to come.

28. **We would never say** there is no such thing as an atheist. For when they knew God…

29. **We would never know** that suffering has a purpose.

30. **We would never know** of the providence of **God.**

31. **We would never know** that Satan is a liar and the father of lies.

32. **We would never know** that Christ Rose From The Grave To Give Us Life.

Read your Bible. It will take you into the world of the unknown.

THE SIGNIFICANCE OF INSIGNIFICANCE

There are people in the Bible that most Christians don't know much about, yet they played a key role in shaping the course of history. Who are these people, and what role in God's redemptive plan did they play? I write this to be an encouragement to those of us who feel we have no significant place in the meta-narrative of biblical history. Yes, the canon of scripture is closed, but God is still writing His story.

Many well-known scholars, pastors, and missionaries came to Christ through the influence of people whose names will never be known. One of the greatest scholars today, Tim Mackie of the Bible Project, was led to Christ over a cheeseburger at Wendy's. His ministry is now world-famous.

Dr. RC Sproul was challenged by some of his college friends to read Ecclesiastes 11:3, which has nothing to do with salvation, but God, through His Spirit, brought him to faith. Imagine what influence Dr. Sproul has had and continues to have as a result of a few insignificant college buddies whom God chose to be very significant?

Because of a snowstorm, Charles Spurgeon's attempt to go to church was diverted, and he stumbled into a little Primitive Methodist church where a preacher read from Isaiah, and a fifteen-year-old Spurgeon was converted. Every Christian knows of Charles Spurgeon, but who knows the name of the preacher?

Billy Graham was a skeptic until he went to a revival and heard evangelist Mordecai Ham. His heart was moved, and he soon surrendered his life to preach. Everyone knows who Billy Graham is, but few know of Ham. The stories are endless of the significance of insignificance.

Do you see yourself as insignificant? Perhaps your insignificance will change the world. Joseph was faithful in prison by asking the prisoners why they were so sad. Had he not asked that question, there would be no Israel through which the Messiah would come. Could God have used another way? Yes, but that is not the issue. The issue is that in His providence, he leveraged the insignificant to bring about the significant.

Could God be using your perceived insignificance to bring about something great? Who knows? You might be close to the next Spurgeon. You are much more significant than you realize, all by His grace.

SPIRITUAL SUICIDE

We've all heard of physical suicide when someone feels so overwhelmed by depression, they choose to end their pain by taking their own life. It's a heartbreaking and tragic situation. But far more tragic is spiritual suicide. This occurs when an individual intentionally dismisses God's clear plan of salvation and opts to determine their own spiritual path, deciding what they believe leads into His Kingdom.

The default mode of the human heart is to believe that my personal standard of human goodness is the standard God requires for entrance into His eternal Kingdom. Let's play this out in real life. Would people visit a restaurant that doesn't list prices on the menu? You want to know your total cost before paying. Essentially, you're interested in knowing the price beforehand.

You head off to college, but first, you check the cost and learn about the grading system. You want to know the standard. We do this every day—whether it's in sports, education, speed limits while driving, the cost of gas, and more. But strangely enough, the one standard very few people even consider is the standard required to enter the Kingdom of God. Why would humanity avoid looking into the most important standard of all? What must I do to be saved? What is the standard of goodness to secure my eternal destiny?

Another big question regarding this issue is, has God given us the standard, or are we left on our own to figure it out? If we are, then we have an even bigger question. What kind of God would call Himself loving, kind, merciful, and desiring that no one would perish while leaving the world in the dark regarding our eternal salvation? What is the standard for entering the Kingdom of God?

Strange as it may seem, man's prideful nature has decided not to consult God but set up religious systems with many hoops to jump through to appease God, who ironically rejects all those hoops.

Scripture has made it quite clear as to why the Bible was written, "To make us wise unto salvation through faith in Christ Jesus" (2 Tim 3:15).

But religion keeps people ignorant of salvation. Religion makes man the center of the story. His ticket into heaven is his spiritual letter sweater. And that sweater displays all the Sunday school ribbons, church attendance, giving, good deeds, and a host of other self-promoting endeavors.

But scripture has another view of the matter. "There is none good, no, not one." There is none who seeks after God, not even one" (Rom. 3:12). Jesus said to the rich ruler, "Why do you call me good?" Jesus answered, "No one is good except God alone." (Mk. 10:18). Either Jesus isn't good, or he is God.

Religion is pride before the law, while

Christianity is humility before the cross

Christianity rests on the finished work of Christ

While religion rests on finishing

The work of Christ.

So, did the Lord leave us in the dark, or did He make us wise unto salvation by being the light of the world?

STORMS IN THE BIBLE

Over the years, I've realized that any topic mentioned repeatedly in the Bible has a deeper story behind it. Tracing blood throughout scripture tells a fascinating story of redemption, along with sin, good versus evil, and a myriad of other subjects.

The subject of storms is no different. There are no multitudes of references, but the ones mentioned tell a story and a significant one at that. I am not trying to say that all these biblical storms relate to the storms in our lives, but there might be a connection well worth pondering.

Storm of Judgment: The first storm is the great flood. I can't even grasp the magnitude of forty days and forty nights of rain that covered the mountains. Here is what we read: "Then the Lord saw that the wickedness of man was great in the earth and that every intent of the thoughts of his heart was only evil continually" (Gen. 6:5).

The Lord had to judge the world because of its wickedness. This is a prelude for future judgment. The Lord does not take sin lightly. Note that the whole world was evil. We are rapidly moving in that direction. I have come to realize that the Lord has a cup of patience that, when full, his judgment comes. I get that from The Flood, Sodom, and Gomorrah, and a statement made in Gen.15:16, which states, "the iniquity of the Amorites is not yet full." I call this the fullness principle. This is when God says, *Enough is enough.*

Storm of Discipline: When the Lord spoke to Jonah about going to Nineveh, and he decided that fleeing from the Lord on board a ship was a better idea, the Lord brought His disciplinary hand by creating a storm. Jonah knew the storm was brought about by his God and made that clear to the men on board who had cried out to their gods to save them. The storm kept raging until Jonah agreed to be thrown into the sea to calm it. This discipline helped Jonah fulfill his calling to preach to the people of Nineveh, but it didn't change his heart. He hated the Ninevites because they were Israel's enemies. However, his prejudice was no match for God's plan.

Storm of Testing: Mark 4:35 through 41 gives us the account of Jesus and his disciples crossing over the sea of Galilee when an unexpected storm arose that swamped the boat. Jesus was asleep when the disciples woke Him and rebuked Jesus for not caring about their safety. Let's not forget that Jesus told them they were going over to the other side. If the creator God of this universe says let's go over to the other side, then you can be sure that is exactly what is going to happen, and no storm can overrule God's plan. However, they were walking by sight and not by faith. This was a perfectly planned test of their faith in the midst of a storm.

The Storm that Reveals Faith: Acts 27 gives us the details of a horrendous storm on the Mediterranean Sea with Paul on board and 275 other men. This storm was so dreadful that they feared the ship would be broken in half. Paul, however, had an appointment to meet with Caesar to stand trial. God sent an angel to let Paul know that this appointment would take place and that all the men would be safe. Paul demonstrated great faith in God's promise that he would meet Caesar, unlike the disciples, who doubted Jesus' promise that they were to go to the other side.

From judgment to discipline to testing to faith, there is a story about storms and what they reveal. I think it is well worth pondering each of these storms and seeing if there is a subliminal narrative the Lord wants us to discover.

WHEN TALENT SMOTHERS CHARACTER

I want to explore the words talent and character with both the younger generation and those who have been misled by the idea that talent can overshadow character. I recently had a brief encounter with a very sharp teenager who was a bit miffed when I questioned the morals of a famous pop star she admired. "You're judging," came the reply. I have been well aware that what used to be called holiness is now called legalism. I have witnessed this decline over the years.

It quickly became clear to me that, in the eyes of the young and even some spiritually mature people, talent often outweighs morality. Like an animal suffocating in quicksand, we can be sucked into the mire of looks, fashion, riches, and the talent of a young pop star while disregarding their character. The enemy has lured us into believing what the world admires.

Who cares if they are promoting, via the stage or social media platforms, sexual ethics that mock biblical truth? Who cares if they dress immodestly and use foul language, as long as they are talented? Who cares if they make sexual gestures in front of thousands of adoring fans who are too young to discern right from wrong, as long as they can hit the high notes?

Some people have talent but no character, some people have character and no talent, and those who have both. No one ever talked about the great carpentry skills of Jesus. Other comments made their way into the public square that highlighted His character and not His talent. "This man speaks with authority and not as the scribes" (Matt 7:28). "Never a man spoke like this man" (John 7:46). Pilot said he could find no fault in Jesus (John 19:4).

We are living in a time when we are drawn to a person's talent, disregarding their character. The character can be smothered under a great voice or acting skills, and those who follow these stars soon take on the character of their idols, and before long, Christ is in the rearview mirror, disappearing as quickly as the sexual revolution accelerates its agenda.

"Evil companions corrupt good morals" (1 Corinthians 15:33).

"He who walks with wise men will be wise, but the companion of fools will suffer harm." (Proverbs 13:20).

My point is not to run the bus over pop stars or Hollywood idols. These people have all been made in the image and likeness of God and should be respected from that standpoint alone. But when their character is in direct opposition to that of Christ Jesus, then we must not be afraid to take a stand, no matter how talented they are.

I am not angry with these pop stars but saddened that they are owned by producers, directors, and managers who are making a killing by marketing them as slaves on the auction block of the stage, which is extremely seductive. Most of them have very troubling lives and often admit to alcohol and drug abuse along with deep depression. Jealousy rages among them as social media stirs the pot to keep the press happy with the latest dirt on these idols of worship.

They must keep the fans happy, and the way to do that is to take more clothes off at the concerts, use four-letter words, and promote the sexual revolution. They appear free, but they are trapped, and their adoring crowds will soon be trapped as well. The web they have woven begins to choke the life out of them. However, the only thing the audience sees is what is promoted: Wealth, fame, fortune, good looks, and sexual freedom. John 10:10 says all these are lies from the enemy who has come to steal, kill, and destroy, and as of this moment, is having a field day. Christ has come that we might have life and have it in abundance.

When we find ourselves defending those who promote immorality because they have great talent, we have officially crossed over into idol worship and will soon embrace what our idol promotes. Psalm 115:8 says, "Those who make them (idols) are just like them, as are all who trust in them." Jesus has a better idea when He said, "You shall know the truth, and the truth will set you free" (John 8:32).

THE CHEERIO PRINCIPLE

The Cheerio principle defines the trajectory of most lives, particularly the wealthy. Allow me to set the stage. A one-year-old is sitting happily in their highchair as mom pours out some Cheerios on the plastic table. This sweet, innocent child loves to share these round little bites of cereal with mom and dad as they walk by. As the child gets older, they start applying some simple math. Keep in mind that all they can say at this point is mama and dada.

Yet their frontal lobe begins to kick into action as algebra, trigonometry, and a bit of calculus are leveraged in their little brain, and voila, their latent selfishness comes alive as they soon begin to realize that "for every Cheerio I give away, that is one less for me." ME, ME, ME!!! Mom leans over for her sweet little child to accept their usual generous offering, only to be met with a clenched fist. No Mine!!

Unfortunately, this principle follows us all the days of our lives. Proverbs 27:20 says, "The eyes of a man are never satisfied." Why is this? Suppose you make one million dollars a year. That is certainly enough to live a comfortable lifestyle. Why not give away three hundred thousand? Because if I do, that second home is now out of reach. If I eventually start making two million a year, then I'm on track to buy a Rolls-Royce. But if I give away five hundred thousand, I can only buy a Lexus. As income grows, the Cheerio principle takes over. From cars to three homes to private jets and islands, there's no limit to our desire for more.

So, when you feel this monster raising its ugly head, just think about the trajectory you will find yourself on. The Cheerio principle takes you away from your family, keeps you at the office longer, staring at a computer screen that has zero personality, and robs you of time that will never be retrieved. This demon of greed will follow you to the grave, maybe even faster than you'd like. Your pillow will be filled with regrets that keep you awake at night. Now is the time to reflect on your life and say goodbye to the endless pursuit of more. There is no pillow soft enough to comfort a guilty conscience.

THE POWER OF LOVE AS EXPERIENCED BY THE ONE BEING LOVED

1 CORINTHIANS 13

Thank you for being patient with me. It gives me a sense of connection with you. And how I so appreciate your kindness, particularly when I don't deserve it. It lavishes me with great joy. You never show envy toward those who have more. Grace is like your teacher, helping me grow into maturity. You never lift yourself up with pride or boastfulness, and because of this, I experience true freedom when I'm with you.

This allows me to experience great freedom in your presence. I'm immersed in a harsh world, but your lack of rudeness resurrects my soul. I am forced to take inventory of my own life. You avoid self-seeking but set a higher standard with all humility of mind by thinking more highly of others than you do yourself. Such virtue affords me great comfort.

I have done many foolish and upsetting things, but you never display anger. This encourages me to be myself and learn from your gentle spirit. By never holding onto past wrongs, I feel no judgment and can find peace, which brings me great comfort. You never delight in evil, and that lifts my soul and spirit daily. You constantly shield me from myself and the harmful influences around me. This is a great comfort when I feel down and lonely.

You are so trusting by providing a safe haven in which to lay my burdens, deepest thoughts, and secrets at your feet. Thank you for giving me such hope, so as to maintain an eternal perspective. Your perseverance helps me stay focused on what really matters—loving supremely. Thank you for loving me unconditionally, for that is everything.

TRIGGERS, TRAUMA AND TOXICITY

We're hearing more and more about people in their thirties and forties who have turned their backs on their parents. We also hear from those in their sixties and seventies, sharing how their children have completely cut them off. They have emailed, texted, or had face-to-face encounters with their parents, saying they want nothing to do with them for the rest of their lives.

This is becoming somewhat of an epidemic. I hear story after story. What is going on here? This didn't exist when my generation was growing up. I suspect there may be a few outliers, but they would be just that: outliers. I loved my parents, and so did my friends. What has changed? Why the sudden shift? Answer? *5 e internet.* Please don't write me off too quickly. The internet, like most of man's inventions, serves good purposes as well as evil ones. Remember, Satan is the prince and power of this present evil world.

The nascent psychology of the modern era is to cast the blame on our parents for all of our spiritual, mental, and physical maladies due to poor parenting. No doubt, many have had traumatic upbringings and are suffering to this day as a result. But the number of those who hate their parents is off the charts. There is an exponential rise in this new drama of life. This humanistic psychology is based on three words: *Trauma, triggers, and toxicity.*

The reason you are suffering is that your parents were hateful people. They ***traumatized*** you by disciplining you and not giving you what you wanted. Your parents are the real cause of all your anxiety. Stay away from them because they are ***triggers*** to all your pain. If you continue to be around them or communicate with them, it will only bring up bad memories of the past. Keep your distance and avoid any contact. They are dangerous. You will only suffer more because they are ***toxic.*** Let them know you will never talk to them again. This toxic relationship, if not cut off, will only spread like a poison in your system and the family tree. Keep your children away as well. This could spread to them and only curse the family line. Be certain to warn your siblings, as we all need to be on the same page.

Before the internet, there was no way to glean all this humanistic counsel, and the parent-child relationship was healthy, but certainly not in every case. I don't wish to paint an unrealistic picture of bygone years. The sinfulness of man has always been, but its accessibility has never been as available as it is today. With the press of a button, you have full access to the demonic world of secular humanistic thought. And such influence can be passed on from one person to another instantly. People continue to feed each other what terrible parents they had. There is the never-ending enforcement of those who are of like mind. They love to compare stories and thus fortify their pain and misery by hearing, "Yeah, my parents did that too."

So, what are we to do? Explain that Adam and Eve were not traumatized. What about Christ? I think when this happens, it is time to have at least a short talk. "Before you walk out on us, I think you at least owe us an explanation." We have a few questions we would like *honest* answers to. What has prompted you to think like this all of a sudden? Why such an unexpected U-Turn in our relationship? Did you come to this decision on your own, or has something like the internet or friends who've also left their parents influenced you? How long have you felt this way? Did your professor at school make you think this? What will the consequences be of such a big decision? Have you thought about how this will affect your life and future generations? When we're gone, will you have any regrets?

This issue has become very important to me. I wish I could stop this overwhelming wave. These are just a few of my thoughts for those of you who have experienced such loss. I praise God that all four of our children love us, each other, and the Lord. All by the grace of God. Don't beat yourself up if your children have turned on you. God, the perfect Father, had two children. Look how they turned out. We are not responsible for how our children turn out. We are responsible for training them up in the nurture and admonition of the Lord (Eph. 6:4). They are morally responsible to take it from there.

GOSPEL ACCELERATION

God's work behind the scenes is laid bare in his providence. Providence is God's ability to take all the good, the bad, and the ugly and bring about His plan. In Genesis 22, we have the offering up of Isaac.

This story is both deeply troubling and incredibly revealing about the gospel, making it one of the most powerful in scripture.

The nameless servants of Abraham are needed for the drama to unfold. Here is what Abraham says to the two men just prior to offering up Isaac. "*Stay here with the donkey while I and the boy go over there. We will worship and then we will come back to you*" (Gen. 22:5. Most people who have a fair understanding of scripture are very familiar with this account. We all know the statement, "We will return," suggests that Isaac doesn't experience death. But we would never know this if the two men were not in the picture. Had they not been there, Abraham would not have revealed what he was thinking. In Hebrews eleven, we are told that Abraham reasoned that God could raise the dead.

The reason the nameless men are so important is that they tie together Genesis 22 and Hebrews 11:19. By using these men, we can see the acceleration of gospel revelation, which picks up blinding speed until the gospel Himself arrives. What a story.

UNDERSTANDING THE WORD SO WE CAN UNDERSTAND THE WORLD

Since sin entered the world, life has been full of struggles. The world tries to escape its challenges by creating a perfect society through human wisdom, which the Lord calls foolishness. In case you haven't noticed, things are not going too well. The main problem is that the foundation for this magnificent society is built on human knowledge and not God's wisdom. When God builds the foundation, it is secure. Hebrews reminds us that no human city will endure but the one that is to come (Heb. 13:14).

Human knowledge is increasing at an exponential rate, and since knowledge is designed to solve problems, the problems should be declining in step with the increase in knowledge. I am aware that I am beating this theme of knowledge vs wisdom to death, but we simply must grasp this vital difference. King David said in Psalm 119:18, "Open my eyes that I might see wonderful things in thy law." And then he says why he is making this request. "I am a stranger on the earth; do not hide your commands from me" (Psa. 119:19). Can you see what he is saying? He has no idea from human intelligence how to understand and navigate this world without God's wisdom and direction.

But we all know that man is failing miserably by denying biblical revelation. This is not happening. Just look at the news, as this is our daily report card, revealing how bad we were the day before. Mankind keeps putting his finger in the dam while trying to hold back the Niagara Falls of gender fluidity, transgender surgeries, pornography in grammar school, drag queens in libraries, gay marriage, pronoun preferences, and a host of other moral maladies.

The finger in the dam is no longer needed since the dam no longer exists. Our government tore down the dam years ago. "The Lord saw how great the wickedness of the human race had become on the earth, and that every inclination of the thoughts of the human heart was only evil all the time" (Gen.6:5). This is where our present society is.

When the first gay marriage was performed, people who were religious and nonreligious were up in arms. Now, they are marching in the streets in celebration of this new depravity. Second Peter chapter two depicts this in detail when it says,

"*These people are springs without water and mists driven by a storm. The blackest darkness is reserved for them. For they mouth empty, boastful words and, by appealing to the lustful desires of the flesh, they entice people who are just escaping from those who live in error. They promise them freedom, while they themselves are slaves of depravity—for "people are slaves to whatever has mastered them" (1Pet. 2:17-19).*

This is where the church enters the scene. We cannot reverse the situation, but we can be salt and light to impede its growth. One of the joys of being a pilgrim is knowing this is not our true home, yet feeling sadness as we witness the struggles of its people. How much do we need to love those who oppose what we stand for?

APPLICATION

Suffering: One of the greatest mysteries in the Christian life. Used by unbelievers to attack Christianity. How could a loving God allow such suffering in the world?

Several things to keep in mind regarding this charge. Does the unbeliever have an answer to suffering? If we evolved, we should have already overcome disease and human cruelty by now. But things are only getting worse.

Suffering is due to sin entering the world. God is not the author of evil, but he did ordain that evil would exist. Sin has corrupted all the world, including nature and various forms of suffering.

If there were no sin, there would be no military, police, FBI, CIA, locksmiths, lawyers, contracts, etc. Sin is big business.

If the Lord answered this question, there would be no need for faith. Most of the people in scripture did not know at the time why they were in pain.

Joseph didn't know at the time why he was being treated horribly. He had done nothing wrong. But later he utters his famous words in Gen. 50:20 "What you meant for evil, God meant for good."

Job never knew why, but at the end he said, "My ears had heard of you, but now my eyes have seen you" (Job 42:5).

Suffering is often a punishment. It can be used to get people's attention. We may bring it on ourselves.

Suffering often brings people into a deeper intimacy with the Lord.

It may also come from spiritual warfare. Satan is a roaring lion seeking whom he may devour. Or persecution.

The only religion where the founder enters into our suffering. That is no small matter.

Judging: Have you ever heard the world say, "Your bible says judge not?"

This comes when we refuse to march in a gay pride parade or bake a cake for a same-sex wedding. We are seen as bigots.

A poll was taken a few years ago with the question, "How does the world perceive Christians?" Guess what the top three were? Hypocrites, judgmental, and anti-gay.

Let's look at Matt. 7:1

There is more to the verse. Jesus goes on to explain what He means.

We are to assume that our log is bigger than the one we are judging. We need to self-examine (Gal. 6:1)

The word for judge is Krino. It means to decide. Jesus is not saying we never decide, but how we decide.

We must assume our vision is impaired. This is a good starting point. Ja. 4:11-12

Ann Woodyard. The blind man. Someone's marriage.

How they raise their kids. The number of factors that enter into the story is manifold.

Yes, we can judge. If a politician states clearly what he or she believes about an issue, then we have the facts.

Forgiving: To forgive means to release a debt. This is not natural. We are, by nature, grudge-holders.

Jesus is the supreme example. Father forgive them. Keep in mind, they did more than just slander His name. They killed Him.

Lord's Prayer. "Forgive us our debts as we forgive our debtors." Jesus paid the debt for the person who wronged you. We want Jesus to forgive us, but not the person who wronged us.

Matt. 18:21-35

Are we doormats? No. Matt18:15

Forgive and forget is bad advice. You can forgive but still avoid the person who hurt you.

Forgiveness takes one, reconciliation takes two.

SECOND OPINIONS ARE NOT ALWAYS WISE

Getting a yearly physical is considered a good thing, and the older one gets, the more often they should get one. At my age, doctors suggest getting one every half hour. It really interferes from tee to green, but that's another story.

The phrase *"getting a physical"* is something we all know, but have you ever heard of getting a *spiritual?* Seems logical to me, since humans are made up of souls and bodies, that both ought to be examined from time to time to see if there might be an unknown physical or spiritual malady not perceived by how well one feels.

Hearing the words, "You have stage four liver cancer," sends a shock wave through your sense of wellness. When your world is turned upside down, the first thing you think of is seeking a second opinion. We care deeply about our physical health and do whatever we can to keep it in good shape. Surely, another doctor will give me better news.

What happens to us when we are given a spiritual and are told our spiritual condition is stage five? We are pronounced dead. *As for you, you were dead in your transgressions and sins, in which you used to live when you followed the ways of this world and of the ruler of the kingdom of the air, the spirit who is now at work in those who are disobedient (Eph. 2:1-3).*

Where does one go to get a second opinion on their death? They are fully aware of their spiritual death because the law is written on their hearts (Rom.2). The Holy Spirit convicts them of sin (Jn 16:9) and their conscience accuses them (Rom.2:15). But our passion to live as we please will always seek a second opinion about our spiritual death, and we are sure to find what we are looking for.

The apostle Paul adds to this by explaining why people seek a second opinion about their spiritual death. They suppress the truth in unrighteousness (Rom.1:18). In other words, the pleasure of their sin is so great that it pushes away what they know to be true and seek another opinion.

If you feel deep down that pornography is wrong, you can always find a psychologist online who will tell you what you want to hear.

"Don't suppress your sexual passions as this will lead to psychological damage, not to mention missing out on all the pleasure passing in review."

If you want to sleep with your boyfriend or girlfriend and feel convicted by your conscience, you can always seek a second opinion. There are plenty out there. "Would you buy a pair of shoes without first trying them on? Why marry someone without first seeing if the two of you are sexually compatible?"

If you know that abortion is wrong but you just don't want the responsibility of caring for a child, you can always find a good argument in your favor, such as, "The nine pound six-ounce protrusion in your stomach is just a mass of tissue," or "a woman has the right to do what she wants with her own body," (strange argument since it is not her body that is being destroyed). Or the government should not interfere with a woman's reproductive rights. (Another strange argument since it sounds like the right to reproduce is being denied). Don't expect arguments to be logical when sin is the subject.

Jesus put it well when He said, "*This is the verdict: Light has come into the world, but men loved darkness rather than light because their deeds were evil. Everyone who does evil hates the light and will not come into the light for fear that his deeds will be exposed (Jn.. 3:19).*

By nature, humans only want a second opinion about their spiritual death if it promises them life. "*You will not surely die,*" the serpent said to the woman (Gen.3:4)."

"*For God knows that when you eat of it, your eyes will be opened, and you will be like God, knowing good and evil (Gen.3:5)."*

The enemy has been offering a second opinion on spiritual death from the beginning, claiming that when you embrace evil, you'll find life. But John makes it clear—there is no truth in him. This is what the sexual revolution parades before the world, promising life but finding death. Jesus has a remedy for this tragic lie when He said to Martha, "*I am the resurrection and the life. The one who believes in Me, even if he dies, will live (Jn. 11:25).* Jesus doesn't give opinions; he distributes truth, and when Jesus speaks, you won't need a second opinion. "For you shall know the truth, and the truth shall set you free."

YOU'RE A MOTHER

You're a mother-and the evidence of this sobering fact bears heavily upon your emotional constitution with every passing day. You've changed diapers, wiped runny noses, cooked ten thousand meals, and washed as many floors as possible. You either have or will experience all the stages attendant to this great title.

The first stage demands your constant attention as your "candle goeth not out by night," explaining that ghosts don't exist or that nightmares are nothing to worry about. Morning arrives sooner than you'd like, with its barrage of verbal protests like "Billy hit me," "David's trying to eat his cereal with a fork!" and "Have you seen my underwear, Mom? Huh? Huh?"

You have learned by experience that facing the music at this early hour is merely the prelude of what's to follow. By nightfall, you have had it. If you hear one more question like "Do worms yawn?" or "Where does the white go when the snow melts?" You'll scream. Each day takes its toll, and you pay it faithfully because you're a mother.

Like a tidal wave, the teen years break upon the shoreline of your life-unannounced and unprepared. You trade in your bib for boxing gloves. New demands and new challenges force your hand. Nursery rhymes won't cut it. You're a counselor whose sensitivity and advice must be couched in love. You're dealing with tender hearts that question self-worth and life's values. The world is pressing in with its agenda. Too much restraint and rebellion may ensue. Too little, and the world swallows another victim. Prayer becomes your ultimate weapon, and a powerful one at that. You stay the course because you're a mother.

As your children leave the nest, you pose for a different picture. You're a grandmother, and this mountain-top experience offers a breathtaking view of the past, the present, and the future. It gives you a chance to experience the contentment of knowing you have helped to landscape the lives of those whom God lovingly calls "The fruit of the womb." You're a bit older and a bit wiser now, and if the truth were known, you wouldn't trade it in for anything. It is for this reason that today and every day, we rise up and call you blessed because you're a mother.

THE PARABLE OF A CHURCH PLANT

Once upon many time, a group of men and women gathered to plant a church in their neighborhood. But this was going to be a church different from all other churches. You see, Happy Church was to be built upon people who were disgruntled with all the bickering and fighting they had experienced in other churches. Happy Church was going to be characterized by love, unity, and sound teaching. Twenty people, ten men, and ten unrelated women, gathered in John's living room to discuss how to pull off that which has never been experienced—true happiness in the church. John opened the meeting with a prayer, which ruffled a few feathers. Who put him in charge? Some muttered to themselves. Why a man and not a woman? Others sighed. But this is Happy Church, so just let it go. John welcomed everyone with a joyful grin and began by asking the gathering if there were any issues that needed to be put on the table at the outset. Nancy, after raising her hand, said, "I assume the five points of Calvinism will be the bedrock of our teaching." There were audible gasps throughout the room. "Surely you are kidding," Tom blurted out. Nancy was quick to find the door, and she left in a huff. "Better off without her," could be heard from some members. John was quick to bring things back to order, and everyone settled back in their seats, knowing that a spirit of divisiveness was now gone. "Are there any serious matters before we move on?" John queried. Tim jumped in and said, "I do hope hymns will be a priority. These silly praise songs drive me crazy with such shallow theology." Martha was deeply offended since she led worship at her last church and used praise songs to reach the younger generation. Visceral expressions of anger began to take over the meeting. John tried to calm things down when one of the members noted a wine rack tucked back in John's study. The volume rose as Pete expressed disdain for alcohol and said he could never be part of a church where alcohol was permitted. Others launched in and called Pete a legalist. Verses for and against wine were being volleyed back and forth. Other issues began to spontaneously surface, and the vitriol was quickly putting a damper on Happy Church, as everyone left very sad.

THE PARABLE OF THE PURCHASE

Four men enter the produce section of a local grocery store. Though none of these men know each other, they are all strong followers of Christ. They travel in different circles and attend different churches, but have an abiding faith that gives them direction and wisdom for living. As they gather around the display of fruit, each begins to make an assessment of what the Lord would have him purchase.

The Charismatic wants to be sure that he is spirit-led. He is mesmerized by the selection and lays hands on the fruit he believes to be anointed. Under his breath, he utters, "Praise Jesus," and heads for the checkout lane.

The Mystic waits patiently for the inner voice of God to direct him. He has a vision of the exact fruit and makes what he is sure is an impeccable choice.

Confident in the sovereignty of God, the Calvinist is assured of making the right selection since it was foreordained before the foundations of the world. He only needs to concern himself with God getting all the glory and the purchase being gospel centered and not moralistic. How could he possibly go wrong with such robust theology?

The Dispensationalist has but one question: "Is purchasing such delectable produce biblically sanctioned prior to the Rapture?" Certain that it is, he reaches for the perfect fruit.

Each man heads to his respective home, rejoicing in what he is certain was a God-ordained purchase, only to be greeted with bad news from his wife, saying the local news channel has sent out a warning that local produce has been contaminated with a dangerous pesticide and is not suitable for consumption.

Disappointed, each man opens the cavernous jaws of his garbage can and watches the contaminated fruit, escorted by gravity, make its way to the bottom, along with some bad theology.

SUPPRESSING THE TRUTH

"For the wrath of God is revealed from heaven against all ungodliness and unrighteousness of men, who hold the truth in unrighteousness" (Rom. 1:18). I believe that Romans chapter one, from verses 16-32, is one of the most important verses in all the Bible. It tells us why people excuse their sinful behavior. Other translations say they suppress the truth or hold down the truth. The sexual revolution suppresses what they know to be true. We all do. It's our nature to shut down our conscience and replace it with lies and excuses. Someone once said, "An excuse is the skin of a lie wrapped with a reason."

The real problem with suppressing the truth over and over is that our conscience stops functioning. The scriptures refer to this as a calloused conscience. I am well aware that we are marinating in immorality as a society. Even though this chapter deals with lost humanity, it can carry over into the world of the church. We can get used to the darkness. When that happens, we lose our sense of hating sin and seeing it as no big deal. When a nation collectively loses its conscience, God gives it over to their own way, as Romans says three times in chapter one. We are our own worst enemy, but we're so blinded we can't see it. When you can't see where you are headed, you can be certain a collision is in your future. Have you looked at our nation lately? We are living in total rebellion against God. When God gives us over to our own way, we find ourselves leaning on our own understanding, which Proverbs tells us not to do (Prov 3:5-6).

This soon becomes God's judgment, which is what we are under at this very moment. Let's make sure we, as the children of God, are not helping to speed up the decay.

WHEREVER YOU GO, YOU'RE GOING TO BE THERE

I know this is not the most enticing read. Stay with me. There is some profound truth in this title. Obviously, wherever I go, I will be there. Give this some thought. Suppose you own a yacht and are suffering from a terminal disease. The yacht will not heal you. Suppose your marriage is on the rocks. Going to Disney solves nothing. My point is that you can't run from trouble. Jesus said, "In this world, you will have tribulation; be of good cheer. I have overcome this world" (John 16:33). We tend to run from reality and the truth.

You can run from the moral presence but not the real presence of the Sovereign God. Movie stars flee to their yachts, Lear jets, and sexual partners, but find themselves in utter despair because these are temporal solutions to eternal problems. The well runs dry.

You can flee from your own conscience, but sooner or later, you will feel its condemnation. Ignore it and you will soon feel nothing. That is usually the result of suppressing the truth. Trouble is on the horizon, and I will visit you shortly. Moving from one place to another never settles the real issue. Fall on your face before a holy God and admit your need for him, and not a new location. Temporal locations fix nothing. Eternal locations are found in the finished work of Christ. Once we find that to be true, all other issues fall into place. Wherever you go, you will be there with all your baggage and that which is stored in the overhead compartment.

Time to stop, take inventory, and see where you are because wherever you go, you are going to be there. Where are you, and what did you bring with you? Let's find our identification in Him. Then and only then will we find our true location.

MODELING

O.K. It's word association time - one of Psychology's favorite games. Here's how we play. I give you a word, and you say the first word that comes to your mind. For example, if I said ball, you might say round; if I said knife, you might say cut; if I said handsome, you might say, Mike Minter - but then again, you might not. Now that you have the idea, let's try one more word - MODELING. Well, what comes to your mind? Glamour? Beautiful People? Fur Coats? The Sears Catalog?

At the risk of being psychoanalyzed, I'll tell you what comes to my mind when I think of MODELING. I immediately think of a model's qualifications. You know - high cheekbones, perfect ratio between height and weight, and as if that weren't enough, add photogenic to the list. Fall short in any area, and "Don't call us, we'll call you" will be the studio's parting words.

Perhaps if I were a bit more heavenly-minded, this word would take on a different meaning. After all, the Bible has a great deal to say about modeling. "...and be clothed with humility" I Peter 5:5. "Put on the whole armor of God" (Ephesians 6:11), "Ye are our epistles written in our hearts, known and read of all men" (II Corinthians 3:2.) "Not the outward adorning... but the hidden man of the heart, which is in the sight of God a great price" (I Peter 3.3).

The beauty of God's modeling program is that anyone can qualify - anyone. I once heard it said that a person can be paralyzed from the neck down and still model the Fruit of the Spirit, "love, joy, peace, long-suffering, gentleness, goodness, faith, meekness, temperance." Joni Erikson Toda comes to mind. If you are not familiar with her story, look it up.

How well I remember my dad modeling honesty by telling a cashier she had given him too much change. And then there was the time I had broken my arm in a car wreck, but my father refused a check from the Insurance Company because our hospitalization was covered by the Military. No doubt your parents or someone you have admired modeled a character quality that you are now able to pass on to your children.

One thing is for certain: You can have family devotions until the swallows come back from Capistrano, but if you don't model it, your children won't buy it, nor will your employees, friends, or neighbors.

So why not slip into something comfortable, like the Fruit of the Spirit - you'll look great, even if you don't have high cheekbones.

MORAL DISCERNMENT

"Wherefore let him that thinketh he standeth take heed lest he fall." (I Corinthians 10:12.)

Few Christians, if any, plan to get themselves into a moral crisis. As much as we have convinced ourselves that we will never be in a car accident or fatal plane crash, we have equal confidence that the strong undertow in the current of moral perversion will never claim us as victims. Yet how shocked we are to find that those holding to our same lofty principles have gone the way of all flesh. We are visibly shaken to hear that Fred and Sally are splitting up or that George is seeing another woman on the side. We are floored to hear that the author of countless books on the family, who has taught in the seminary classroom and lectured throughout the world, has been leading a double life. His traveling companion is his homosexual partner.

Christians never expect this will happen to them. After all, we have the Good Housekeeping Seal of Approval stamped on our soul. No Christian looks to the future and plans to get divorced or commit adultery. Who in their right mind wants to become an alcoholic, drug addict, or thief? Nevertheless, it happens, and with far greater regularity than we would like to admit. Why? Because the exemption's wall surrounds only those who know they are not exempt.

Many men have walked through the doors of my office and said these familiar words: "I never thought it could happen to me." But it did, and along with the tears, the questions started to pour out. "How can I prove to my family that I still love them?" "Will my wife ever forgive me?" "Can our relationship ever be the same?" It offers little comfort to quote our opening verse about "taking heed lest we fall" when infidelity has left its mark.

Somewhere in the past, man has adopted the idea (for the sake of mental comfort) that such sins and their attendant consequences only happen to the other guy. Perhaps it stems from the fact that none of us has a realistic appraisal of ourselves. somehow, youthful lusts don't war against our souls. life has a better script, and such Tales of woe are reserved for our next-door neighbor. We are exempt! As Lot looked over the plains of Sodom, would his wildest dreams have carried him to a cave where the last chapter of his life would be stained with drunkenness and incest? When David strolled the rooftops, did he foresee a scenario of adultery and murder? A man after God's Own heart? never! had they been warned, would their Cry of exemption have been, "It could never happen to me?" Without moral discernment, it may be said of us as it was of David, "Thou are the man."

WORDS TO LIVE BY

"Can't you do anything right? You mindless idiot, how could you have forgotten the car keys? That's the third time this week you've spilled the milk!" Like the relentless pounding of the surf, waves of criticism wear on the beachhead of the soul.

It should be no surprise that low self-esteem leads to a list of mental maladies. Is it any wonder that the word "can't" is so quick to volunteer its services in dampening the spirit of any endeavor? As it steps from the ranks of our vocabulary, it proudly wears the uniform of failure - and why not?

We have been reminded countless times of our limitations and inadequacies. Should we not have anticipated a down generation - one that has been nurtured by sarcastic speech and vitriolic verse? But praise God, the reverse is equally true. Words of praise and encouragement lift the spirit and strengthen the soul.

"A wholesome tongue is a tree of life: But perverseness is a breach in the spirit." Proverbs 15:4

"A word fitly spoken is like apples of gold in pictures of silver." Proverbs 25:11

"Let no corrupt communication proceed out of your mouth, but that which is good to the use of edifying, that it may Minister Grace unto the hearers." Ephesians 4:29

Let's be openly candid for a moment. (Anything much longer might be too painful.) Do you criticize more than encourage? Don't feel bad; I, too, was visited by the spirit of conviction and found wanting. By the way, he won't leave until he has accomplished his mission.

So, let's take time to meditate on the above verses. They should be waiting in the wings of our minds for many daily performances. You might anticipate an encore, for people love to be around those who encourage - so plan on a full house.

Well, I hope this has lifted your spirits and strengthened your souls. You are exciting, wonderful people.

Well, 2024 is Past Tense. As with most years, the ledger sheet will reflect both the good and the bad. I suspect it won't go down as the most eventful year in human history, but no doubt some of her chapters will be dog-eared from future fingers researching the past. Be assured, 2024 will not rest in peace - as historians are noted for performing autopsies on bygone eras.

As far as headlines are concerned, this past year has distinguished itself as the year of a failed presidency and more hatred between the two parties.

On the International Scene, Terrorism has accelerated. But all of this is mere Human History passing through the narrow corridor of time. When I speak of "Human History," I mean the vast numbers of lost humanity moving aimlessly about this Globe. As Christians, however, we have a different perspective. We look beyond our natural horizons and see the Sovereign Hand of God at work. "Though we see through a glass dimly,"(1 Cor.13:12), we are assured that the confusion on Planet Earth is the natural consequence of sin. We are not taken by surprise when we observe man's futile attempts to improve life through materialism or technology. We know better - God, and He alone, is the only answer to life and its attendant problems.

However, I never cease to be amazed at the number of Christians who have become absorbed by the World System. If 2024 were not spiritually fruitful, I would challenge you to take 2025 by the jugular - sometimes, it is the only way to get attention.

ENCOURAGEMENT

Much like any challenge, however, the effect is usually short-lived and fades quickly into the mist of our memory. Before this happens, let's bring this giant to his knees, where we can face him eyeball to eyeball.

Why We Need To Encourage And Be Encouraged

1. Because through much tribulation, we must enter into the kingdom of God: We all need to be stroked by the warm hand of encouragement. Who can you think of that just might need some right now?

2. Because we receive far more criticism than praise, our emotional ledger sheet tells the truth. It sure would be nice to get it to balance before the final account. You can help make a difference!

3. Because it develops friendships: We naturally seek out those who refresh us with words of comfort rather than those who destroy us with words of criticism.

4. Because it gives health to the recipient: Pleasant words are as a honeycomb, sweet to the soul, and health to the bones." Proverbs 16:2

5. Because we hurt far more deeply than we will admit. Most people carry burdens the weight of which cannot be estimated by an outsider. Learn to encourage when you sense a need.

How To Encourage

1. Learn to encourage daily: Remember—a person's self-worth hangs on the thin thread of encouragement, and some are at the end of their rope. Don't wait to give words of comfort.

2. Learn to relate to those who have similar needs: Be sensitive to those who are going through a trial similar to what you have already experienced. How did you weather the storm? Let them know how God used that difficulty in your life.

3. Learn to be a good listener: We all need to learn to read between the lines. People rarely unload their problems all at once. They usually deliver them in small packages just to see if you're concerned enough to

open them. If you do, they will likely make another delivery. No one will expose their deeper feelings to people who show little or no interest. Be a person who cares!

"It will never be the nature of a man to encourage, but it will forever be his need."

REMINDERS

Reminders - they're nasty, tactless, and vicious. They can be rude, crude, and downright ugly. They mock us at every turn and strike without warning. They're unwanted guests who view us as vacant lots in which to set up shop. From age spots to bald spots, from Dr. Shoal's foot pads to orthopedic Nikes, the handwriting is on the wall – "Age is getting the upper hand." A reminder we would just as soon forget.

An innocent remark that you're "getting a little thin on top" strikes deeper than you want to admit and serves as another reminder that you're no spring chicken. An old college yearbook brings back the days when you wore a size 6 dress. Without hesitation, this tactless intruder tells you your present size is somewhere between your phone number and zip code - and another reminder bears its teeth like an angry canine.

Insensitive as they are, reminders will blitz if given the opportunity. Been to the nursery lately? The kids who used to occupy the playpens are preparing for college boards. Yet, with a sigh of bewilderment, we quote those all too familiar words, "My, how time flies."

Reminders - why don't they just leave us alone? Why don't they go back to the pit where they belong? Why don't they stop plaguing us night and day with the philosophy that "our cup is not half full but half empty?" How does scripture suggest we handle these professional irritants? Proverbs tells us "As a man thinketh in his heart, so is he." (Prov 23:7). Not bad advice. Maybe we ought to change our frame of reference. Is it really all that bad that we're getting older? We're also getting a lot wiser. Life doesn't play as many tricks on us as it used to. We're able to sense that "something is rotten in the state of Denmark" well before we enter its gates. The ebb and flow of the world system is somehow more predictable and no longer takes us by surprise.

Sure, the kids will be grown and gone before we know it. But is it really all that bad? I must admit I look forward to the days when my tribe comes home for the holidays. And guess what? There will be all kinds of reminders in our home. Pictures on the wall, photo albums, and slides that have frozen time will tell the story of days gone by. We'll laugh together and rib each other over fond memories. We'll hold hands at the table, and perhaps a bit more firmly, as we thank God for His goodness. A kiss on my bald spot will be followed by a few "one-liners" from my offspring as our clan demonstrates a healthy sense of humor inherited from a home where reminders don't rule but serve. I wrote those words back in the seventies. They have come true, and my cup's not half empty or half full – it runeth over.

GUIDELINES FOR PRAYER

Too often, we take a verse of Scripture at face value without considering the rest of God's revelation on the matter. Take prayer, for example. John 14:14 says, "If ye shall ask anything in my name, I will do it." Nothing could be clearer. If I ask for anything and tack on the name of Jesus, then God is obligated to come up with the goods. Experience alone would show this not to be true.

Since we, as a corporate body of believers, are asking God to supply the necessary funds to put up a facility, it only seems right that we follow His guidelines for prayer as revealed in other parts of Scripture.

1. "If I regard iniquity in my heart, the Lord will not hear me" (Psalm 66:18). God turns a deaf ear to those who harbor sin. So, take some time this week to examine yourself.

2. Ye ask, and receive not, because ye ask amiss, that ye may consume it upon your lusts (James 4:3). Will your request glorify God? If not, don't ask for it!

3. "And whatever ye shall ask in my name, that will I do" (John 14:13). Notice carefully the three little words in my name. They are not so little! Simply stated, don't ask for anything that Christ wouldn't ask for. When we don't know what to pray for, the Holy Spirit will intercede (Rom 8:26).

4. "If ye abide in me, and my words abide in you, ye shall ask what ye will, and it shall be done unto you" (John 15:7). When God's Word abides within us, it gives us direction for intelligent prayer.

If the above guidelines are followed, then our request will not be in vain.

So, pray in his name, believing, with a clean heart, abiding in his word, not greedy in our request, that God may be glorified. Now, we can take John 14:14 at face value.

LIFE IN THE FAST LANE

I'm not exactly sure to whom this should be addressed, but if it strikes a responsive chord, maybe I'm playing your song. I heard an interesting illustration on the radio a few weeks back. It was one of those little seed thoughts that take root within your grey matter and won't let go until you cry, uncle. Well, I've tried uncle and aunt, been through my family tree, and to the phone book, but to no avail. I'm writing this as a last-ditch effort in hopes that this plaguing thought will flow from pen to pad. So here goes.

The illustration? Well, it has to do with Progeria. _Pro who? Progeria. It's a baffling childhood disease. What's the cause? Unknown. Its symptoms? Rapid aging. Its consequences? Early death. Children at the age of ten look to be in their sixties or seventies. Their life expectancy is short. They have, in fact, physically experienced all of life in just a few short years. What a tragedy!

There is an interesting parallel between Progeria and a disease that many young people experience in the moral realm. Its name? Life in the fast lane. Its cause? Peer pressure. Its symptoms? Moral impurity. Its consequences? Early burnout! Many children, six or seven years of age, know every four-letter word in the book. By the time they are ten, they may have sniffed a little glue or taken a few drags of marijuana. Premarital sex refuses to play second fiddle and strikes a major chord in the early teenage years. Gone are the days when dad sat down to explain to his teenage son the facts of life. Anytime much past the age of seven, and you're a little late, pop. What a sad commentary on our society.

So, what's it going to be? Life in the fast lane with the in-crowd, or life on the cart path with the One who said, "Straight is the gate and narrow is the way" (Matt. 713-14). No doubt you remember the story about the tortoise and the hare. Remember who won? Guess what? They live longer, too.

BALANCED COMMITMENT

Commitment is one of the most intimidating words in the English language. It's demanding, restrictive, convicting, and challenges even the most disciplined individuals. It tightens the noose around the neck of anyone who contemplates its meaning.

As much as we shy away from this three-syllable drill sergeant, just try and live without its ten letters tattooed to your soul. Nothing of any value can stand in its absence. No child will ever grow up to tickle the keys of a Steinway unless commitment is etched into his character during the early years of practice. Nor will gold medals grace the neck of sluggards- just ask Mary Lou Retton. Wars are not won in moccasins but in the well-worn boots of commitment. Governments fall, businesses fail, and families blend into oblivion when this virtue is not within the rank and file of priorities.

What disturbs me, however, is not the lack of commitment but the imbalance of it in our lives. People are committed to work but not wedlock, the house but not the home, and golf but not God. We are so highly disciplined, but only in those areas that we deem important.

The scriptures offer a balance to this much-needed character builder. "Whatsoever you do, do all the glory of God" (1Cor. 10:31). That's devotion to God. "As for me and my house, we will serve the Lord" (Josh. 24:15). That's a dedication to the home. "If a man doesn't work, neither shall he eat" (2Thess 3:10). That's discipline on the job.

Anything out of balance experiences either pressure or tension. When work crowds out time with the family, pressure builds within the home. When hobbies and leisure put God on the back burner, expect a little heat from heaven; remember--pressure and tension are internal reminders that our commitment is either out of balance or invested in areas that have no real lasting value.

Commitment shouldn't be a taskmaster but an escort.

If the truth were known, most of us have our commitments out of balance, which is perhaps why our lives are out of whack. The scriptures are replete with illustrations on commitment, but the one I cherish most is the CROSS.

A REMEDY FOR WORRY

Worry, fear, and doubt never assert themselves until challenged. As a matter of fact, we are not even aware of their potential until there is a threat to our security. As soon as these unwanted visitors arrive, we ask ourselves where they've been hiding. Like a dormant seed that comes to life as soon as it feels the warmth of the sun, these pesty rascals come out of hibernation when notified that a bill is due, a job is threatened, or a spot on the lung appears. These fiery darts from the wicked one rob us of the joy of the Christian life and can only be quenched by taking up the shield of faith.

Imagine what thoughts must have flooded the mind of Noah (no pun intended) when he was warned "of things not seen as yet." What will the world be like after this judgment? How will we eat? Where will we live? But Noah found grace in the eyes of the Lord, and Hebrews 11:7 tells us he did it by faith.

With social security worse than it is now, Abraham must have been tempted to question God's providence in giving him a son at age 100. How will we provide? What will the schools be like in Canaan? Will he be affected by heathen playmates? Again, relief is spelled F-A-I-T-H. "For whosoever is born of God overcometh the world, even our faith" (1 John 5:4).

It's time to admit that this fearsome threesome has plagued us long enough. It seems they are no longer just visiting but have found a permanent resting place in our minds. Like an old hound who has a favorite spot by the fire, these denizens from the pit have decided to stay for a while. Timothy reminds us, however, that "God has not given us the spirit of fear, but of power, love, and a sound mind" (1 Timothy 1:7).

So, let's trust in the one who has power over our emotions and fears. Spend time in His Word. It's amazing the healing power that scripture brings to those who allow it to take root. Luke chapter 8 tells us that God's Word is a seed - so let's do some planting today - you will never regret the harvest.

THE SPIRITUAL GOLD

As much as I enjoy watching the Olympics, there are several aspects of these time-honored games that disturb me. First - the pressure to perform within certain distance and time parameters seems a bit unfair. There are no second chances, no manana, it's now or never. Ice skating is a prime example., In pairs figure skating, you are given two minutes and fifteen seconds to prove to the world that you are the best. For an imaginary moment, let's step out onto the ice and feel the heat. The world is watching. Thousands of dollars and as many man-hours of practice have brought you here for this moment. Don't blow it! A hush falls over the crowd as the music begins.

You have been here before, but only in your dreams. What trophy room would best display the Olympic gold? How would you handle all the publicity? What would it be like to be called the best in the world? But you're no longer dreaming - you're on the ice, and the first two minutes of your performance have been flawless. There are just fifteen seconds between you and the gold medallion you have waited for and worked for all your life. Suddenly, there's a split-second lapse of memory on the part of your partner, and a required critical spin is overlooked. It's too late; the music is unforgiving, and so are the judges. There's no grace, no forgiveness, no tomorrow. Your hopes and dreams have been dashed against the rocks of misfortune. It's all over.

Exaggeration? Hardly. Just ask Randy Gardner. Eight years ago at Lake Placid, Randy pulled a muscle during a practice session and was unable to compete. It was a nightmare. The red, white, and blue would not be hoisted that afternoon. A pulled hamstring silenced the National Anthem.

My second concern regarding the Olympics has to do with the selection of sporting events. Who decides what sports qualify to be included in the Olympics? Have you seen the luge? Don't get me wrong - I like the luge. But let's be honest. How can you be considered the best in the world at a sport that only eight people in the world have ever heard of? Out of those eight, only four have access to a practice course.

And you really have to question the sanity of the driver. There he is, lying on his back, traveling at 75 mph down an icy labyrinth. The winners always have names like Yen Yenson or Egor Pordanski. If I decide to compete in the next Olympics, where can I practice? Did you know there is not one luge course in all of Tennessee? Not one! I hope Yen's mother doesn't read this.

My third and final gripe, and wouldn't you know it, has to do with the sponsors. Every product known to man is the official product for the Winter Olympics. Budweiser is the official beer, and M&M's is the official snack food. Come on! Can't you just see these physically fit, alpine athletes chasing down M & Ms. with a Bud? The world never ceases to amaze me.

So, what does all this have to do with a pastoral challenge? Just this. Paul drew a great many examples from the Olympic Games of his day to drive home spiritual truths. "Know ye not that they which run in a race run all, but one receiveth the prize? So run that you may obtain. And every man that striveth for the Mastery is temperate in all things. Now they do it to obtain a corruptible crown, but we are incorruptible" (1 Corinthians 9:24-25).

Do we strive for perfection? Do we lay aside every weight and the sin that doth so easily beset us? And isn't it a comfort to know that our performance doesn't have to be flawless? His grace is always sufficient to forgive. And there is always a second chance - just ask Jonah.

THE SLUGGARD

"How long wilt thou sleep, o sluggard? When welt thou arise out of thy sleep?" Prov 6:9 Proverbs plumbs the depths of the Sluggard's laziness and concludes that he needs to "go to the ant and consider her ways" (Prov 6:6).

Who isn't familiar with this guy? He is a professional at explaining why the job didn't get done. He hates the clock. It's a formidable foe, and the conviction from the chronometer is more than he can bear. It reminds him of deadlines that he never meets. It tells him that he has slept long enough and it's time to rise, but he can't because he is "hinged to his bed" (Prov 26:14). Life is just one big siesta. Time is never on his side but always on his back. Excuses for unfinished projects abound. He talks of work, but the horsepower of his mouth is never translated to his hands. He is idle, lazy, slothful - he is, in fact, a sluggard!

A casual glance at Proverbs will show that God has no small dislike for laziness. Diligence is exalted as a virtue and should transcend every area of our lives. When diligence rains in eating, one is able to say no to the cake that calls, the pie that pleads, the bread that begs, or the dessert that dares. When diligence is not at the Helm of the home, then the hand that could turn the wrench turns on the tube, and in the wake of such decisions lie unfinished projects, still unfinished. When diligence is lacking in business, the seeds of procrastination take root, and the fruit of delay is not far from Harvest – "the boss is gone," "it can wait till tomorrow," or "it's not all that important anyway."

Unfortunately, the saddest Sluggard has not yet been addressed. He is not easy to spot. As a matter of fact, he is paradoxically disguised by his diligence. He is diligent in his business and works well around the house. The shine on his car and the well-manicured lawn will testify to this. But he is a slugger. His Bible would flinch with pain if it were ever opened. That is - if he could find it. His prayer life is virtually non-existent. When asked to do something for his Sovereign rather than to praise himself, the former is dismissed with the ever-present excuse, "I'm too busy," and God is again placed on the back burner. But that's okay - He can take the heat. The question is - can the sluggard?

WHY TOMORROW IS MORE VALUABLE THAN TODAY

Can I actually prove this title to be true? Let's see where such logic takes us. The economic law of supply and demand says that when a product is scarce and the demand is high, the price goes up, and the reverse is true as well. Sand is not as valuable as diamonds for one simple reason: its supply far exceeds its demand. That being true, then the days of our lives fit neatly into this economy. Each day that passes means we have fewer days left of our lives. When there is a scarcity of days, they become more valuable with each passing day.

At eighty, I give a lot of thought to the passing of time. Each day is more valuable than the previous day. That doesn't mean that today is a better day in terms of health and happiness, but in terms of the shortage of days left. The Psalmist said, "So teach us to number our days that we may apply our hearts to wisdom (Psalm 90:12). But how can we number our days if we don't know how many we have? James reminds us not to presume upon the future (4:13). The Psalmist must be talking about today because it is the only day we have hope since we are still alive. In other words, use your time and days wisely. The Apostle Paul spoke of redeeming the time for the days are evil (Ephesians 5:16), and they still are. The farther you go back in history, the greater the skill and productivity in art, music, architecture, mathematics, and sculpture. Why? Because people were prodigious in their use of time. Very little entertainment existed. Politicians had extensive talent in diverse disciplines. There are no political figures of the last hundred years that compare with Jefferson, Franklin, and the signers of the Declaration of Independence. There will never be another Beethoven, DiVinci, Michelangelo, Newton, Galileo, and a thousand others. We have become time wasters and gluttons for entertainment. I point no fingers as I am guilty as well. Most of us are.

What kind of legacy do we want to leave the next generation? That we conquered Candy Crush? Time is not a respecter of persons. I'm writing my third book, and others have written fifty books. Comparison may not be the wisest thing to do, but let's face the facts: they have as many hours in a day as I do. So, let's not lose the central theme of these few paragraphs. Life is short, eternity is long; invest heavily in the latter.

THE ANATOMY OF CONFLICT

Church work certainly has its challenges. But this is true in all walks of life. Many years ago, we had a couple who didn't get their way and caused a real stir. As the conflict began to spread, I decided not to waste this opportunity. I began to study how it spread, the stages it went through, and the damage it caused. Here is what I observed.

1. An offense occurs.
2. A biased view of the offense is shared with friends.
3. Friends take up the offense.
4. Sides begin to form.
5. Suspicion on both sides develops.
6. Each side looks for evidence to confirm its suspicion. You can be sure they will find it.
7. Exaggerated statements are made.
8. In the heat of conflict, those involved hear things that were never said and say things they wish they had never said.
9. Third parties, no matter how well-intentioned, can never accurately transfer information from one offended party to the other.
10. Past offenses unrelated to the original offense surface.
11. Integrity is challenged.
12. People call each other liars.
13. Those who try to solve the problem (e.g., church leadership) are blamed for not following the proper procedure and become the new focus.
14. Many are hurt.

When the flames became embers, I realized that in the midst of conflict, people say things they wish they had never said and hear things that were never said. Few remain calm, and even fewer want to hear the facts.

GOLF AND CHRISTIANITY

What kind of a title is Golf and Christianity? A number of years ago, I realized that all sports were fascinating, each having unique pressures. I love to watch great athletes perform at the highest level, whether it be the Olympics, March Madness, the Super Bowl, or the World Cup. I am struck by the sheer ability these otherworldly beings possess.

But and I don't mean to offend, golf is in a completely different category. It is an island completely separated from the mainland for all other sports. I didn't say it is better or harder than other sports, but in a totally different league. Is the athleticism in golf at a higher level than in other sports? No! Do professional golfers practice harder? No! But I can prove beyond a shadow of a doubt that golf is The Lone Ranger of sports. Are you ready for the simple answer? The answer comes in the form of a question. How many football jokes are there? How many baseball jokes are there? How many tennis jokes are there? Practically none. How many golf jokes are there? Hundreds upon hundreds. Most of them have to do with the addictive nature of the sport. There is the one about a foursome crossing a road that went through the course. As a funeral procession passed by, one of the golfers took off his hat and put it over his heart. His playing partners commented on what a sweet gesture that was, to which he responded, "This Thursday would have been our thirtieth wedding anniversary."

All the jokes are along those lines. So, how does golf relate to Christianity? Golf is separated from all other sports, and Christianity is separated from all other religions, not because of jokes but because of grace. Every religion in the world dictates some type of moral or ethical behavior needed to enter Heaven, Nirvana, or the Happy Hunting Grounds. Even some belief systems under the umbrella of Christianity mix works and grace. Christ plus my church attendance, or how many good deeds I have done. Biblical Christianity is Christ alone.

So, the next time you take a backswing, just remember it's the only sport that represents the gospel. I guess that's just par for the course.

BLOODSTREAM

I heard a scholar years ago say that once evil enters the bloodstream of a society, it is virtually impossible to remove it. I began to think of that statement found the following to be true. Here is the trajectory it takes. From

Shock

to Toleration

to Acceptance

to Embracing

to Promoting

Clark Gable, in 1939, used the word damn in Gone With The Wind. The world of unbelievers was shocked as the producer had to pay $5000 to the Motion Picture Production Code Office for the use of that word. $5k then is equal to $113,000 today. The average movie today, if fined, would pay about $11,000,000, and that's for a fairly clean film.

This is clearly a downward spiral, as Romans 1 declares. The sexual revolution makes Gone With The Wind look like a child's Sunday school class. Society quickly becomes accustomed to evil because we are soaking in it every day. It will worsen, as scripture predicts.

GUARD YOUR HEART

"Trust in the Lord with all thine heart and lean not on thine own understanding. In all thy ways acknowledge him, and he shall direct your paths. Be not wise in thine own eyes: fear the Lord and depart from evil" (Prov. 3-6).

When it comes to the power of verses, this is a fifty-megaton bomb. Many have memorized it. Believe me, I know firsthand. So, when I am raking leaves, do I need spiritual advice? No, I need a little grit and muscle. Leaning on your own understanding has to do with moral and ethical fleshly inclinations. They say if it feels good, do it. If a lie will get me out of trouble, why not lie? These are powerful inclinations that, if obeyed, will yield serious consequences. But we have to know his word in order to know his will so as to avoid leaning on our own understanding. These verses are worth meditating on for the rest of your life. Those leaning on their own understanding are being discipled by a fool.

Every temptation to lie, cheat, or steal comes from our fallen nature, the enemy, and the world. We must be alert daily to the schemes of the evil one. Do we really believe that he seeks to devour us according to the Apostle Peter and to steal, kill, and destroy according to the Apostle John? Anytime we lean on our own understanding, we become targets of the enemy. Guard your heart at all times.

ENOUGH IS ENOUGH

How many times have we heard the three words enough from politicians and civic leaders following a serious threat that has been made to our society? Racism, a school shooting, violence in the streets, or other disasters always trigger these famous three words, yet apparently, enough is not enough. When will enough actually be enough?

I have always wondered why unbelievers and often believers continue to believe we are on the verge of erasing enough. That will not happen this side of heaven. There will always be wars and rumors of wars.

When Christ returns, enough is enough will be replaced by the One who truly is enough.

Heard not judged

People want to be understood before they are found guilty by those around them. No one likes the gavel dropped on their reputation before they can plead their case. There was a great deal of slander swirling around the Apostle Paul for preaching a false message. He had to stand before one political leader after another to clear his name. All of us have had our names dragged through the mud and felt the sting of a slanderous whip across our naked backs. We so desperately want to defend ourselves, but the platform has been removed, and we live with the pain of a sullied reputation. Everyone faces this in life, and there is no escape route. But keep in mind that as much as we despise being falsely accused, so do those we falsely accuse.

I'm particularly sensitive to this. When I was at the Naval Academy in the early sixties, my dad was the previous Superintendent. There was a professor who thought I was getting special treatment. So he decided to alert the news about this, and it became a scandal. My name was in the Washington Post, Time magazine, Newsweek, and on Walter Cronkite's evening news. I was famous for being a sleazeball. Talk about hurt. So be certain to listen before you pass judgment.

Give up your right to being offended.

There is a bit of irony when it comes to this subject at Christmas. The Prince of Peace has arrived, and there are more hurt feelings over these holidays than at any other time of year. "No one ate my corn casserole, and I spent so much time preparing it." "I dished out more on my parents than they spent on me." Come on now, admit it. Few escape being offended at Christmas.

"Great peace have they which love thy law: and nothing shall offend them" (Psa. 119:165). I was at a seminar fifty years ago, and the teacher asked everyone to give up their right to being offended. It was one of the best decisions I have ever made. Ministry is the place for this Psalm to be employed. Not sure I would have survived. No Private can criticize a General, nor a player criticize a coach, nor an employee criticize the CEO, unless he wants a Court Marshall, be benched, or fired. But anyone can gossip and even slander their pastor with impunity. The parishioner can't be benched. They are free to roam and spread the latest news that you have lost your step in the pulpit. Your preaching is getting a bit shallow. There is no way to stop the trafficking of such gossip. Once you give up your right to being offended, the sting may not go away, but it has less effect.

Several thoughts on how I have dealt with this over the years. 1) Did they mean to hurt me? Probably not. Few people get up in the morning with the intent to hurt someone. 2) Was I overly sensitive? Most likely the real issue. 3) They intentionally wanted me to be hurt. That person is no friend and not worth dealing with. I hope this helps, because life is filled with offenses. I most likely have offended you somewhere in this book. Now you know what to do.

Challenge

One of the chief objectives through these pages of my thoughts distilled is to challenge you to take time to think. I mean, take a long walk and consider what you have to offer the Kingdom that will lift up and encourage. Don't let your thoughts be wasted. I realize this book has a strong slant toward the Christian community, but trust it will bless all who read it.

THE HERMENEUTICS OF HERMENEUTICS

Hermeneutics is the science of interpreting the Bible. But what is the science of interpreting hermeneutics? Who is the infallible interpreter? Throughout the ages, there have been endless scholars debating text after text. This has led many an atheist to employ this argumentative spirit as ammunition against the church. It has confused countless believers, as many have chucked the faith.

Obviously, the Lord is not the author of confusion (1 Cor.14:33). So, who is? The enemy has thrown the church into a cauldron of endless interpretations of the scriptures. This is found in the world of medicine. One oncologist says operate, another says chemo, another says radiation, and another says eat more veggies. When it's your health, this is a serious matter. How about your spiritual health, which is far more important?

Well, what do you think it means?

If there is one issue that drives pastors and theologians crazy, it's the aforementioned question. Spiritual heartburn ensues. Ten people in a bible study with no theological training could arrive at most any conclusion on a text. So what? Put ten theologians in a room with the same text and out come the swords of church history, hermeneutics, original language, dispensationalism, and covenant theology. Sparks fly everywhere, and yet all systems seem to produce the same fruit. But we can't see the forest for the trees. The underground church in China has no access to seminary training or original language studies, yet it is growing faster than anything in the US.

The most unlikely verse in all the Bible to reach a person with the saving knowledge of Christ is (Eccl 11:3), which states the following: "If clouds are full of water, they pour rain on the earth. Whether a tree falls to the south or to the north, in the place where it falls, there it will lie."

The late great theologian Dr. RC Sproul read that verse and said, "I'm the tree that is rotting. I need a savior," and was converted. Go figure! That verse has nothing to do with salvation, but the Spirit of God illuminated the mind of RC, which led him to Christ. Leading theologians get a hall pass when it comes to hearing from God. Many a missionary has been called to the field through verses that have nothing to do with missions. Read Faithful Women And Their Extraordinary God by Noel Piper. You guessed it, that is John Piper's wife. The Reformed camp is very leery of visions, dreams, and being led by verses taken out of context, yet that is what her whole book is about.

A little more than fifty years ago, I heard an audible voice say, "Quit your job and teach the Bible the rest of your life." I was thirty at the time, and I am now 81. The only time I have a check in my spirit about someone hearing from God is when the voice teaches heresy or the person has a history of fraudulent interpretations. When a mature believer says, "I heard from God," I'm all ears. Some may ask you sarcastically, "Was it a bass or a baritone voice?" To which you reply, "Neither, it was a spiritual voice and those that have ears to hear, let them hear" (Matt. 11:15).

So, when you open your bible, say these words. "Open mine eyes, that I might behold wondrous things out of their law (Psa. 119:18). If it was good enough for David, it should be good enough for us.

SPIRITUAL ENTROPY LEADS TO SPIRITUAL ATROPHY WHICH LEADS TO SPIRITUAL APATHY

Unless you studied engineering or a scientific discipline related to the above, you may have never heard of entropy. I looked up a simple definition for those of us who are unfamiliar with this world of science. "Entropy is a lack of order or predictability; gradual decline into disorder." In other words, if you never repair what is broken, your roof, car, or finances will move to disorder. You must put energy into the system, or it will become rubble over time. This includes your marriage, but I digress.

If we took the time to read a journal of a fifteen-year-old in the seventeenth century, the vocabulary would be well beyond that of a present-day Harvard law student. Just read some old Civil War letters written by uneducated soldiers to their families, and you will see what I mean. The penmanship we can't even reproduce today. This is entropy in education, vocabulary, and overall knowledge. So, does this apply to the church? I'm afraid it does. Sermons from yesteryear make the best of preachers today look like they don't know what the Bible is. After years of preaching, a good dose of the Puritans makes me want to crawl into a hole, but then again, they didn't have cell phones. And therein lies the problem.

Instant access to commentaries, podcasts, and great sermons from the best of today has replaced personal study and time in deep meditation. If we want to know what Dr. Thunderbolt thinks about a particular text, then just go to his website or hitch a ride on YouTube, and voila, you have all you need. You hardly lifted a finger, and your brain got a little smaller. Entropy and atrophy are normally pejorative terms. Together, they conspire to remove prayer, meditation, and solitude and keep us busy scrolling through endless foolishness on our phones. Yes, I am guilty! Presently, I am fasting from scrolling as a result of two good friends holding my feet to the fire.

They want me to feed my soul on the Word and not what others say about the Word. There are wonderful books on the Bible, but they are still not the Bible with all its purity.

I had a professor in Bible college who used to say, "It's amazing how much light the Bible sheds on all those commentaries."

So set some time aside and devour the Scriptures. You will be glad you did.

www.ingramcontent.com/pod-product-compliance
Lightning Source LLC
Chambersburg PA
CBHW051144120626
46547CB00012B/940